GRADES **6-8**
MATH

TABLE OF CONTENTS

S0-ADO-888

Connections to Standards

This chart shows the national mathematics standards covered in each chapter.

NUMBER AND OPERATIONS	Standards are covered on pages
Understand numbers, ways of representing numbers, relationships among numbers, and number systems.	9, 13, 16, 19, 22, 26, 30, 32, 36, 44, 47, 65, 70, 72, 75, 78, 80
Understand meanings of operations and how they relate to one another.	9, 13, 16, 19, 22, 26, 30, 32, 36, 44, 47, 65, 70, 72, 75, 78, 80
Compute fluently and make reasonable estimates.	9, 13, 16, 19, 22, 26, 30, 32, 36, 44, 47, 65, 70, 72, 75, 78, 80

ALGEBRA	Standards are covered on pages
Understand patterns, relations, and functions.	34, 36, 39, 42, 44, 47
Represent and analyze mathematical situations and structures using algebraic symbols.	34, 36, 39, 42, 44, 47
Use mathematical models to represent and understand quantitative relationships.	34, 36, 39, 42, 44, 47
Analyze change in various contexts.	34, 36, 39, 42, 44, 47

GEOMETRY	Standards are covered on pages
Analyze characteristics and properties of two- and three-dimensional geometric shapes, and develop mathematical arguments about geometric relationships.	50, 52, 54, 57, 60, 62, 78
Specify locations and describe spatial relationships using coordinate geometry and other representational systems.	50, 52, 54, 57, 60, 62, 78
Apply transformations and use symmetry to analyze mathematical situations.	50, 52, 54, 57, 60, 62, 78
Use visualization, spatial reasoning, and geometric modeling to solve problems.	50, 52, 54, 57, 60, 62, 78

MEASUREMENT	Standards are covered on pages
Understand measurable attribute of objects and the units, systems, and processes of measurement.	57, 60, 65, 68, 70, 72, 75, 78
Apply appropriate techniques, tools, and formulas to determine measurements.	57, 60, 65, 68, 70, 72, 75, 78

978-1-4129-5926-1

GRADES **6-8**

MATH

ENGAGE THE BRAIN GAMES

MARCIA L. TATE

CORWIN PRESS
Classroom

For information:

Corwin Press
A SAGE Company
2455 Teller Road
Thousand Oaks, California 91320
CorwinPress.com

SAGE, Ltd.
1 Oliver's Yard
55 City Road
London EC1Y 1SP
United Kingdom

SAGE India Pvt. Ltd.
B 1/I 1 Mohan Cooperative
Industrial Area
Mathura Road, New Delhi
India 110 044

SAGE Asia-Pacific Pvt. Ltd.
33 Pekin Street #02-01
Far East Square
Singapore 048763

Printed in the United States of America.

ISBN: 978-1-4129-5926-1

This book is printed on acid-free paper.

08 09 10 11 12 10 9 8 7 6 5 4 3 2 1

Executive Editor: Kathleen Hex
Managing Developmental Editor: Christine Hood
Editorial Assistant: Anne O'Dell
Developmental Writer: Karen P. Hall
Developmental Editor: Lisa Collette
Proofreader: Mary Barbosa
Art Director: Anthony D. Paular
Design Project Manager: Jeffrey Stith
Cover Designers: Monique Hahn and Lisa Miller
Illustrator: Yvette Banek
Cover Illustrator: Corbin Hillam
Design Consultant: The Development Source

DATA ANALYSIS AND PROBABILITY	Standards are covered on pages
Formulate questions that can be addressed with data, and collect, organize, and display relevant data to answer them.	22, 72, 80, 82, 85, 86, 89
Select and use appropriate statistical methods to analyze data.	22, 72, 80, 82, 85, 86, 89
Develop and evaluate inferences and predictions that are based on data.	22, 72, 80, 82, 85, 86, 89
Understand and apply basic concepts of probability.	22, 72, 80, 82, 85, 86, 89

PROBLEM SOLVING	Standards are covered on pages
Build new mathematical knowledge through problem solving.	32, 70, 72, 82, 85, 86, 89
Solve problems that arise in mathematics and in other contexts.	32, 70, 72, 82, 85, 86, 89
Apply and adapt a variety of appropriate strategies to solve problems.	32, 70, 72, 82, 85, 86, 89
Monitor and reflect on the process of mathematical problem solving.	32, 70, 72, 82, 85, 86, 89

REASONING AND PROOF	Standards are covered on pages
Recognize reasoning and proof as fundamental aspects of mathematics.	34, 70, 72, 85, 89
Make and investigate mathematical conjectures.	34, 70, 72, 85, 89
Develop and evaluate mathematical arguments and proofs.	34, 70, 72, 85, 89
Select and use various types of reasoning and methods of proof.	34, 70, 72, 85, 89

COMMUNICATION	Standards are covered on pages
Organize and consolidate mathematical thinking through communication.	9, 13, 16, 26, 30, 70, 75, 82, 86, 89
Communicate mathematical thinking coherently and clearly to others.	9, 13, 16, 26, 30, 70, 75, 82, 86, 89
Analyze and evaluate the mathematical thinking and strategies of others.	9, 13, 16, 26, 30, 70, 75, 82, 86, 89
Use the language of mathematics to express mathematical ideas precisely.	9, 13, 16, 26, 30, 70, 75, 82, 86, 89

Introduction

Think back to your years as a student. Which classes do you remember the most? Many of us fondly remember those dynamic classes that engaged our attention. However, we can just as easily remember classes in which lectures seemed to last forever. The difference is that we can usually recall something we *learned* in the dynamic classroom. This is because our brains were engaged.

The latest in brain research reiterates what good teachers already know—student engagement is crucial to learning. Scientists have found that the use of games to energize and engross students is one of the best strategies to activate learning. Can students really learn content while playing games? Walk by a classroom where students are playing a game and you might see chaos at first glance. Look again—this is actually collaboration. Amidst the buzz of competition, students are willingly discussing material once considered bland. When students are allowed to "play," they interact using all of their senses, stimulating brain function that helps retain content.

Every student has his or her own motivation and attitude about math, so maintaining interest is not always easy. But in order for students to truly acquire and retain math knowledge, they must be actively engaged in learning. Games are ideal for this purpose.

How to Use This Book

Correlated with the national mathematics standards, this book provides games that will engage all students, even reluctant learners. The games review concepts in number and operations, algebra, geometry, measurement, and data analysis and probability. They also follow a format that promotes learning and retention: focus activity, modeling, guided practice, check for understanding, independent practice, and closing. These strategies ensure that students are active participants in learning, not passive bystanders.

You may adjust the games to best meet the needs of your students and your curriculum. Games such as Gin Rummy Geometry and Conversion Match-Up may be modified to include pairs or sets of any math concept. Games such as Outdoor Algebra, Math Quiz Show, and Math Baseball are ideal for reviewing entire units of study.

Games can be fun, lively, and spirited. The little bit of extra effort it takes to implement games into your curriculum will reap loads in student involvement. Just like the fond memories you keep of that dynamic class years ago, your students will remember the fun they had in your class and, more important, what they learned.

978-1-4129-5926-1

Put It Into Practice

Lecture and repetitive worksheets have long been the traditional method of delivering knowledge and reinforcing learning. While some higher-achieving students may learn from this type of instruction, educators now know the importance of actively engaging students' brains if those young minds are to truly acquire and retain content, not only for tests but for a lifetime.

The 1990s were dubbed the Decade of the Brain because millions of dollars were spent on brain research, helping educators and researchers alike understand more about the learning process in a young mind. But learning theories that address the importance of actively engaging the brain have been proposed for decades, as evidenced by research such as Howard Gardner's theory of multiple intelligences (1983), Bernice McCarthy's 4MAT Model (1990), and VAKT (visual, auditory, kinesthetic, tactile) learning styles theories.

I have identified 20 strategies that, according to brain research and learning styles theories, appear to correlate with the way the brain learns best. I have observed hundreds of teachers—regular education, special education, and gifted. Regardless of the classification or grade level of the students, exemplary teachers consistently use these 20 strategies to deliver memorable classroom instruction and help their students understand and retain vast amounts of content.

These 20 brain-based instructional strategies include the following:

1. Brainstorming and Discussion

2. Drawing and Artwork

3. Field Trips

4. Games

5. Graphic Organizers, Semantic Maps, Word Webs

6. Humor

7. Manipulatives, Experiments, Models

8. Metaphors, Analogies, Similes

9. Mnemonic Devices

10. Movement

11. Music, Rhythm, Rhyme, and Rap

12. Project-based and Problem-based Instruction

13. Reciprocal Teaching and Cooperative Learning

14. Role Play, Drama, Pantomime, Charades

15. Storytelling

16. Technology

17. Visualization and Guided Imagery

18. Visual Presentations

19. Work Study and Apprenticeships

20. Writing and Journals

This book features Instructional Strategy 4: Games. While playing games, students use teamwork, interpersonal skills, and movement, and experience the spirit of competition. They actively express emotions, interact with friends, and explore new challenges of learning with immediate feedback and success (Beyers, 1998). The inherent joy of play is the brain's link from a world of reality to the development of creativity. In addition, play speeds up the brain's maturation process with built-in elements of competition, novelty, acknowledgement, and time limitations (Jensen, 2001).

Games involve active learning. The games in this book help students learn on a variety of levels. Some games involve quiet concentration, some energized, kinesthetic movement. However, all of the games involve interpersonal skills of sharing, discussing, creating, and working effectively with a team or partner. Once students are familiar with how a game is constructed, they can use these same ideas to create their own versions of the game. Brain research shows that when students are involved in the design and construction of a learning game, the game's effectiveness is enhanced (Wolfe, 2001).

Students are no strangers to competition. They face it regularly— vying for chair placement in orchestra, playing team sports, or auditioning for the school play. That same sense of competition and teamwork can take place in the classroom. Board games, card games, memory games, trivia games, and games that encourage physicality, using the senses, and imagination all provide the social stimulation, discussion, movement, and creativity that make students actively participate in learning.

These memorable strategies help students make sense of learning by focusing on the ways the brain learns best. Fully supported by the latest brain research, the games presented in this resource provide the tools you need to boost motivation, energy, and most important, the academic achievement of your students.

CHAPTER 1

Number and Operations

Spin the Order

Objective

Students will use the order of operations to simplify and solve equations.

Materials
- Spinner reproducible
- Spin the Order reproducible
- pencils
- large paper clips

In this game, students spin a number wheel to fill in missing numbers and simplify and solve a multi-step equation. Their goal is to get a final answer greater than their opponent's answer. Students use both the order of operations and logical reasoning to help them win the game.

1. Write the following equation on the board, and review with students how to use the order of operations to solve it: $12 - (7 + 4) \times 2 = ?$ (Answer: –10) Ask students to list the order of operations rules *(PEMDAS): Solve inside the **p**arenthesis first, then **e**xponents, then **m**ultiply or **d**ivide in order from left to right, and then **a**dd or **s**ubtract in order from left to right.*

2. Give each pair or trio of students a **Spinner reproducible (page 11)**, a paper clip, a pencil, and copies of the **Spin the Order reproducible (page 12)**, one for each player.

3. Show students how to make the spinner by writing a different number in each section, and then using a paper clip and pencil to spin for numbers to complete the equations on the game sheet. Students may write any kind of rational number in the sections of their spinner (integers, decimals, or fractions). Once they write a number on one of the lines, they may not remove it. Their goal is to write an equation that results in a final answer that is greater than their opponent's. The player with the most points at the end of the game wins.

4. Review the rules with students and check for understanding. If needed, review how to add, subtract, multiply, and divide positive and negative rational numbers.

5. Monitor students as they play the game. Check that they are following the rules and are using the correct order of operations. Encourage them to check each other's work.

6. Conclude the activity by inviting students to share their results and discuss the different strategies they used, such as using greater values to multiply or add and using smaller values to divide or subtract to get the greatest answer.

Variations of the Game

- Play a team version of the game, giving each team the same incomplete equation written on a sentence strip. Then give teams one minute to place number cards (numbers written on index cards) in the blank spaces to make an equation with the greatest possible answer. Have teams write their equations on the board and work together to solve them. Repeat with other equations and number cards.

- Have students play the game independently by spinning the spinner to fill in the incomplete equation and then simplify and solve the equation. Have them recheck the equation to see if they could have used a different number arrangement to come up with a greater answer.

- Invite students to write their own multi-step equations for the game. You might also suggest that they include absolute values and algebraic expressions.

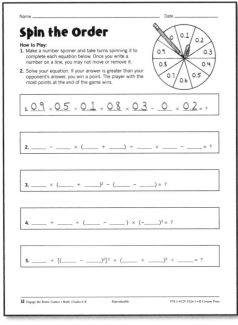

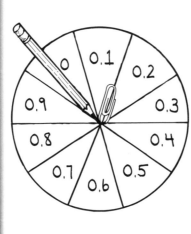

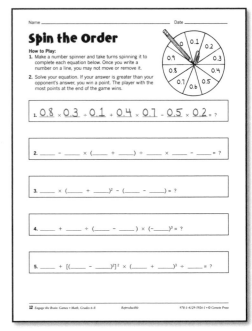

Spinner

Directions: Write a different number in each section of the spinner. Use a pencil and paper clip to spin numbers for the game.

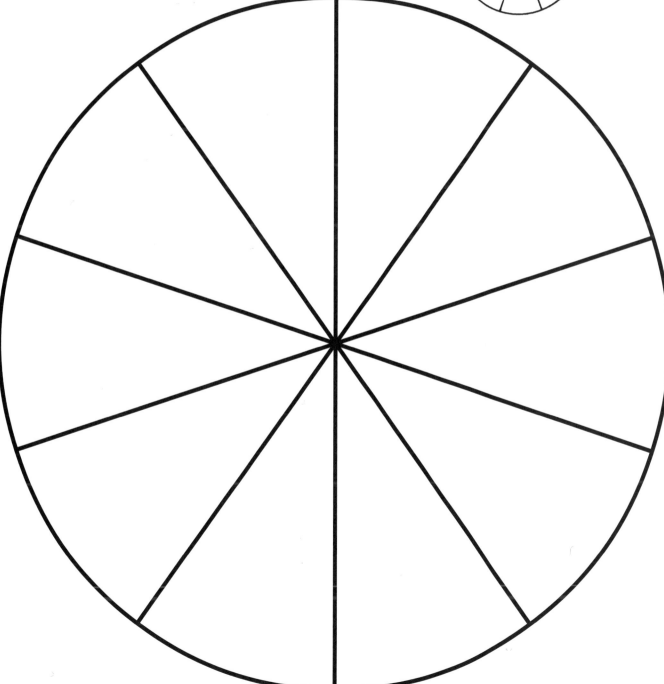

Spin the Order

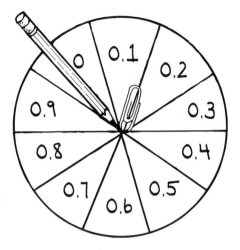

How to Play:

1. Make a number spinner and take turns spinning it to complete each equation below. Once you write a number on a line, you may not move or remove it.

2. Solve your equation. If your answer is greater than your opponent's answer, you win a point. The player with the most points at the end of the game wins.

---

1. _____ × _____ ÷ _____ + _____ × _____ − _____ × _____ = ?

---

2. _____ − _____ × (_____ + _____) ÷ _____ × _____ − _____ = ?

---

3. _____ × (_____ + _____)^2 − (_____ − _____) = ?

---

4. _____ + _____ ÷ (_____ − _____) × (−_____)^3 = ?

---

5. _____ + [(_____ − _____)^2]^2 × (_____ + _____)^3 ÷ _____ = ?

 978-1-4129-5926-1 • © Corwin Press

Last Number Standing

Objective

Students will create and solve multi-step equations and identify different combinations of operational computations that equal the same amount.

In this game of strategy and skill, players take turns crossing off combinations of numbers that equal a given number. The player who uses the last number or leaves only one number on the game grid wins.

1. Display a copy of the **Last Number Standing Game Grid reproducible (page 15)**, and use a bag of number cards from 1 to 100 to demonstrate how to play the game.

2. Divide the class into two teams to play a whole-group version of the game. Have students from each team take turns drawing a card from the bag and crossing off a combination of numbers on the game grid that when added, subtracted, multiplied, or divided, equal the number on the card. For example, they could cross off *2, 11,* and *12* for the answer *46* by using the equation *2(11 + 12) = 46*. Have each team use a different-colored marker to cross off their numbers.

$$12$$

$$46$$

$(30 \times 4) \div 10 = 12$ $2 (11 + 12) = 46$

3. Encourage teams to discuss their solutions and write their equations on the board. Point out that they may use the numbers on the game grid as whole numbers, fractions, or exponents, and they may use any combination of those numbers.

4. Continue playing the game, putting back the chosen cards or leaving them out of the game. Remind students to consider different possible combinations for each answer card they select. Point out that the goal is to leave only one number on the game grid. The team that does so wins the game.

5. Monitor students as they play the game. Remind them to use the order of operations when writing and solving their equations. You might also suggest that they use a calculator to check their opponent's equations.

6. After playing the game as a class, have students play the game in pairs or trios, using another copy of the Last Number Standing Game Grid and their own set of number cards. Have them write and solve the equations in their math journals.

7. After students play a few games, invite them to discuss different strategies that they used during the game.

Variations of the Game

- Have students play independently, keeping track of how many turns they need to get to the final number on the game grid. Have them write and solve their equations in their math journals.

- Ask students to place a decimal point in front of each number on the game grid and on their number cards to play a decimal version of the game. You might also have them include both positive and negative numbers by writing a negative sign in front of some of the numbers on the cards.

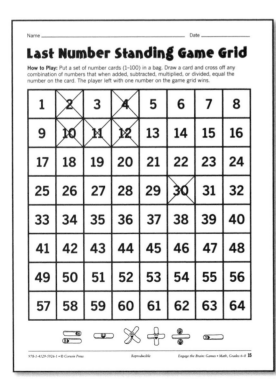

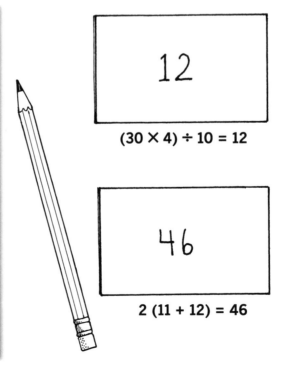

$(30 \times 4) \div 10 = 12$

$2(11 + 12) = 46$

Name _____   Date _____

Last Number Standing Game Grid

How to Play: Put a set of number cards (1–100) in a bag. Draw a card and cross off any combination of numbers that when added, subtracted, multiplied, or divided, equal the number on the card. The player left with one number on the game grid wins.

1	2	3	4	5	6	7	8
9	10	11	12	13	14	15	16
17	18	19	20	21	22	23	24
25	26	27	28	29	30	31	32
33	34	35	36	37	38	39	40
41	42	43	44	45	46	47	48
49	50	51	52	53	54	55	56
57	58	59	60	61	62	63	64

Fill and Win

Materials
- Fill and Win reproducibles
- Spinner reproducible
- pencils
- large paper clips
- calculators

Objective
Students will add, subtract, multiply, and divide real numbers and then estimate which arrangement of numbers to use to win the game.

In this challenging number game, students use estimation and computation skills to determine the greatest possible product or quotient. They must use their knowledge of multiplication and division to help them strategize.

1. Write *1, 2, 3, 4, 5, 6* on the board, and invite students to suggest a four-digit by two-digit number arrangement that results in the greatest possible product. Point out that they can use estimation to help them find the answer. Have students solve each problem and use a calculator to check their work. For example:

Estimate			Exact
$6{,}543 \times 21$	$6{,}500 \times 20$	$130{,}000$	$6{,}543 \times 21 = 137{,}403$
$5{,}432 \times 61$	$5{,}400 \times 60$	$324{,}000$	$5{,}432 \times 61 = 331{,}352$
$6{,}412 \times 53$	$6{,}400 \times 50$	$320{,}000$	$6{,}412 \times 53 = 339{,}836$
$5{,}421 \times 63$	$5{,}400 \times 60$	$324{,}000$	$5{,}421 \times 63 = 341{,}523$

2. Repeat for division, pointing out that the smaller the divisor the greater the quotient. For example: $6{,}543 \div 12 = 545.25$.

3. Give each pair of students one or both of the **Fill and Win reproducibles (pages 17–18)**, a Spinner reproducible (page 11), and a paper clip and pencil for the spinner. Read the directions aloud, and review how to make the spinner. Point out that Round 3 and Round 4 include mixed numbers, with large boxes for the whole number and small boxes for the numerator and denominator.

4. Monitor students as they play the game. Afterward, ask volunteers to share their results and discuss the strategies they used to win.

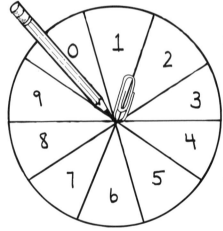

Fill and Win: Multiplication

How to Play: Make a number spinner using numbers *0–9*. Take turns spinning the spinner to fill in each digit of your equation. You may not move the digits after you write them. The player with the greatest product wins.

Player 1: _____ **Player 2:** _____

Round 1

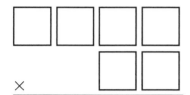

Round 2

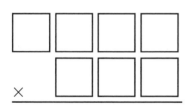

Round 3

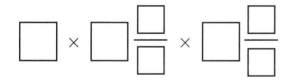

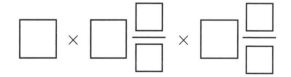

Round 4

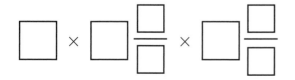

Name _____ Date _____

Fill and Win: Division

How to Play: Make a number spinner using numbers *0–9*. Take turns spinning the spinner to fill in each digit of your equation. You may not move the digits after you write them. The player with the greatest quotient wins.

Player 1: _____ **Player 2:** _____

Round 1

Round 2

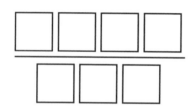   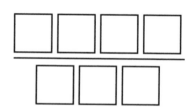

Round 3

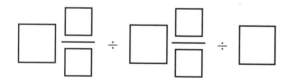   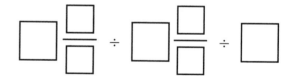

Round 4

Target Zero

Objective

Students will add positive and negative decimals along a number line to reach zero.

Materials
- Target Zero reproducible
- Number Cubes reproducible
- cardstock
- scissors
- tape
- game markers (e.g., colored counters, paper squares)

In this game, students roll their way to zero by adding positive and negative decimals. They will get the opportunity to experience firsthand the inverse relationship of positive and negative values on a number line.

1. Display a number line from −5 to 5 with increments of 0.5. Review with students how to add positive and negative numbers, such as 2.5 + (−1.5) = 1.0, moving to the left on the number line for negative addends and to the right for positive addends.

2. Give each group of two to four students a copy of the **Target Zero and Number Cubes reproducibles (pages 20–21)** copied onto cardstock and different-colored counters for game markers. Demonstrate how to cut out and assemble each number cube.

3. Explain that the goal of the game is to be the first player to land exactly on zero by starting at +5 or −5. Players must decide which number cube to roll each turn and then add their way to zero. If students overshoot, they must use the other number cube to move in the opposite direction.

4. Monitor students as they play the game, making sure they are adding positive and negative decimals correctly. If they finish early, have them play again by adding, subtracting, multiplying, and dividing to get to zero.

Variations of the Game

- Have students create their own version of the game by drawing their own intersecting number lines and using different intervals of numbers along each line.

- Have students omit the number lines altogether and just use different number cubes to add, subtract, multiply, or divide their way from 100 to 0.

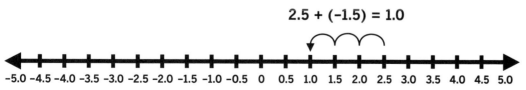

$$2.5 + (-1.5) = 1.0$$

Target Zero

How to Play: Put your marker on –5 or +5 on either number line, with each player starting on a different number. Take turns rolling the positive or negative number cube and adding that amount to move your marker along the number line. If you overshoot, you must use the other number cube to move in the opposite direction. The first player to land exactly on zero wins!

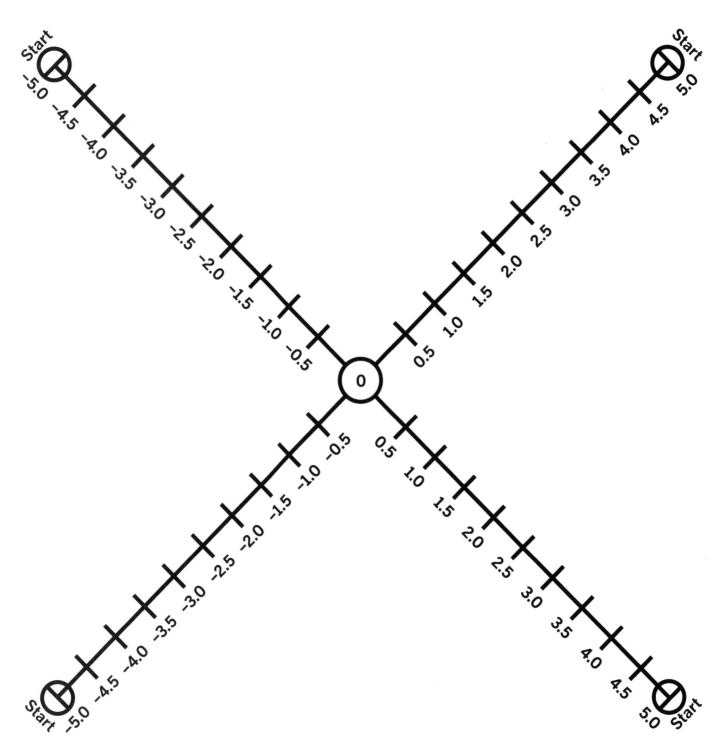

Number Cubes

Directions: Cut out, fold, and tape along the edges to make each number cube.

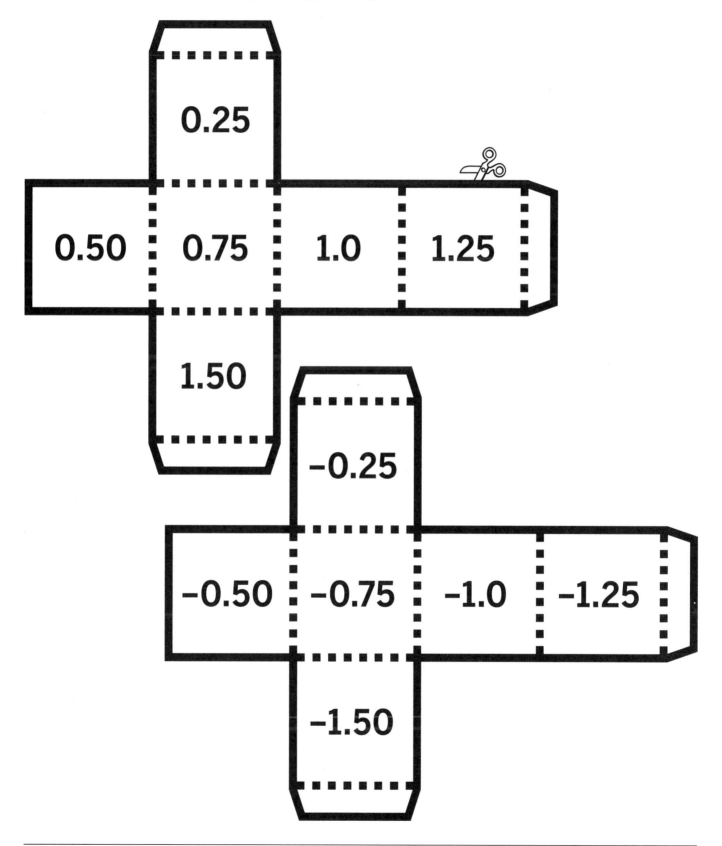

Bowling for Numbers

Materials

- Bowling Scorecards reproducible
- overhead projector and transparency
- empty 1-liter water bottles (10 per team)
- tennis balls or other similar balls
- permanent marker (optional)
- masking tape (optional)

Objective

Students will calculate and record bowling scores in a data table using whole numbers, decimals, or fractions.

In Bowling for Numbers, students use computation skills and a specific method of scorekeeping to calculate cumulative bowling scores. They can play either a regular version of the game, in which each bowling "pin" they knock down is worth one point, or they can play a modified version using decimals and fractions.

1. Have students bring in empty one-liter water bottles to use for "bowling pins" (ten per set). Demonstrate how to place the bottles in a triangular formation, as in regular bowling. If the bottles fall over too easily, add a little water to weigh them down.

2. Give each group of two to four players a copy of the **Bowling Scorecards reproducible (page 25)**, and use an overhead transparency to demonstrate how to score a bowling game. Check for understanding as you explain the rules.

Goal: The goal is to knock down ten bowling pins set up in a triangular formation by rolling a ball from a distance of about ten feet.

a. Each turn or "frame" of the game consists of players rolling their ball twice to try to knock down all ten pins, earning one point for every pin knocked down.

b. Players write the score for their first roll in the top-left corner of the "frame box." They write the score for the second roll in the top-right mini-box of the frame box. They write the cumulative sum (the sum of the two scores plus the prior score) below both scores, in the lower part of the frame box.

c. After each turn, players reset the ten pins for the next player to take a turn.

Name	1		2		3	4	5	6	7	8	9	10	Total
Teddie	5	4	2	6									
		9		17									
Maria	3	5	5	2									
		8		15									

d. Then explain to students how to score:
  - A *spare* is the result of knocking down all ten pins using both rolls of the ball. Draw a diagonal line (/) in the mini-box instead of writing a number. To get the score for that frame, wait until your next turn and add ten points to the score for the *first* roll of that turn (ten plus the score of the next roll). Then add that sum to your cumulative score. Write the total in the lower part of the frame box for the spare. Then continue with your second roll.
  - A *strike* is the result of knocking down all ten pins with the first roll. Instead of writing a number in either corner of the frame box, draw an X or color in the mini-box. To get the score for that frame, wait until your next turn and add ten points to the score of *both* rolls of that turn (ten plus the scores of the next two rolls). Then add that sum to your cumulative score. Write the total in the lower part of the frame box for the strike. Use the same two-roll scores for the current frame, writing your scores in the top-left and top-right corners of the frame box and adding the sum to the cumulative total score.
e. The player with the greatest cumulative total after ten frames wins the game.

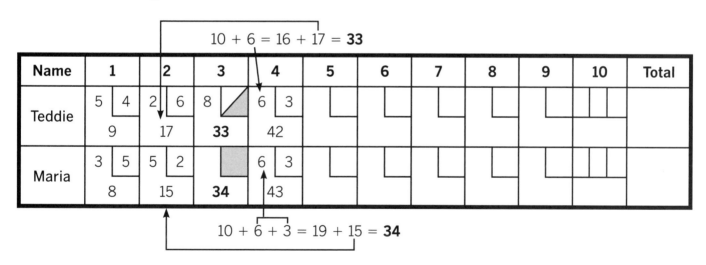

3. Discuss possible ways to modify the game, and give students the option of playing either a regular version or a modified version. For example, instead of having each bowling pin worth one point, have each pin worth 0.1 point, 1/10 point, or any variety of values that total one point or ten points for the entire set. You might also include positive and negative numbers. Use a permanent marker

and masking tape to mark the value on each pin. If the total value of all ten pins is one point, then the value of a strike or spare is +1 instead of +10. For example:

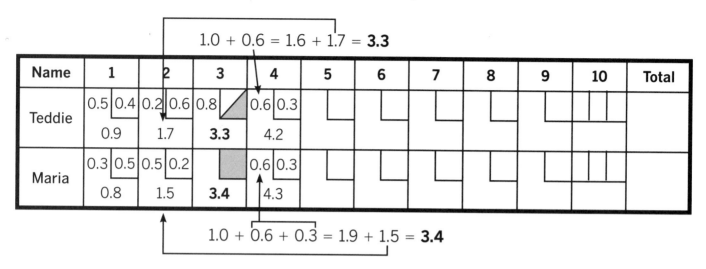

$1.0 + 0.6 = 1.6 + 1.7 = \textbf{3.3}$

Name	1		2		3		4		5	6	7	8	9	10	Total
Teddie	0.5	0.4	0.2	0.6	0.8		0.6	0.3							
	0.9		1.7		**3.3**		4.2								
Maria	0.3	0.5	0.5	0.2			0.6	0.3							
	0.8		1.5		**3.4**		4.3								

$1.0 + 0.6 + 0.3 = 1.9 + 1.5 = \textbf{3.4}$

4. Monitor students as they play the game outdoors or in the gym. Have them mark the "throw" line using any kind of marker (e.g., chalk, tape) and set their bowling pins in a triangular formation, with the pins about one foot apart from each other. Also check that they are scoring their game correctly and resetting the pins after each frame.

5. After the game, invite students to share their results. Encourage them to share the strategies they used to knock down as many pins as possible.

Variations of the Game

- Instead of rolling a ball, have students toss a beanbag to knock down the pins.

- Have students play Bowling for Dollars, with each pin worth a designated money amount.

- Have a bowling tournament to find the best bowler in your class or the school.

Bowling Scorecards

Sample Scorecard

Name	1	2	3	4	5	6	7	8	9	10	Total
Marco	4 5 / 9	2 ◢ / 20	1 2 / 23								
Ana	▨ / 18	7 1 / 26									
Ellie	– 2 / 2	9 – / 11									

▨ Strike   ◢ Spare

Name	1	2	3	4	5	6	7	8	9	10	Total

Name	1	2	3	4	5	6	7	8	9	10	Total

Fun with Fractions

Materials

- Fraction Speedway reproducible
- Spinner reproducible
- counters or handmade mini racecars
- large paper clips
- pencils

Objective

Students will identify equivalent fractions and find the sum, difference, product, and quotient of fractions and mixed numbers.

The following fraction games include Fraction Speedway and Fraction Tic-Tac-Toe. Students will use their math skills (and a little bit of luck) to win each game by identifying equivalent fractions and finding the sum, difference, product, or quotient of fractions and mixed numbers.

Fraction Speedway

1. Give each group of two to four players an enlarged copy of the **Fraction Speedway reproducible (page 28)**, counters for game pieces (or have them make their own mini cars), and a copy of the Spinner reproducible (page 11) with the sections labeled *1/4, 1/3, 2/3, 3/4, 3/5, 1/4, 1/3, 2/3, 3/4, 3/5*. Review with students how to use a paper clip and pencil to spin the spinner.

2. Read the directions of the game together. Players take turns spinning the spinner and moving to the next equivalent fraction on the racetrack. If a player chooses an incorrect fraction, he or she must go back to the previous spot and miss a turn. The first player to reach the finish line wins.

3. Tell students to check each other's choices to make sure their opponents are moving to the next equivalent fraction on the racetrack and not skipping past one or choosing one that is not equivalent. Remind students that both the numerator and the denominator of equivalent fractions change by the same multiple or divisor. Explain that if a player moves to an incorrect fraction, he or she must go back to his or her previous space and skip a turn.

Variation of the Game

For an extra challenge, have students record all of the fractions they land on during the game. Ask them to add all the fractions to see who has the greatest total at the end of the game.

Fraction Tic-Tac-Toe

Materials
- Fraction Tic-Tac-Toe reproducible
- paper lunch bags
- scissors
- index cards (optional)

1. Give each student pair a copy of the **Fraction Tic-Tac-Toe reproducible (page 29)**, and review the rules of the game. (If needed, explain how to play regular Tic-Tac-Toe.)

2. The goal of the game is to be the first player to get three *X*s or three *O*s in a row horizontally, vertically, or diagonally. Students can accomplish this by solving the problems from the game cards and then marking those correct answers on the Tic-Tac-Toe game board (drawing either an *X*—Player 1 or an *O*—Player 2).

3. Practice some examples on the board before students play on their own. Point out that the three games increase in difficulty, and that one card in each game is an extra problem (there are ten cards but only nine answers shown). If a player chooses that card, he or she will not get to mark an *X* or *O* for that turn.

4. Monitor students as they play the game and offer help as needed. Make sure they put only one set of game cards in the bag at a time (play only one game at a time).

Variation of the Game

Extend the learning by having students create their own version of the game to exchange with another pair of students. Have them write their own set of problems on index cards and draw their own Tic-Tac-Toe game board of answers to use for the game.

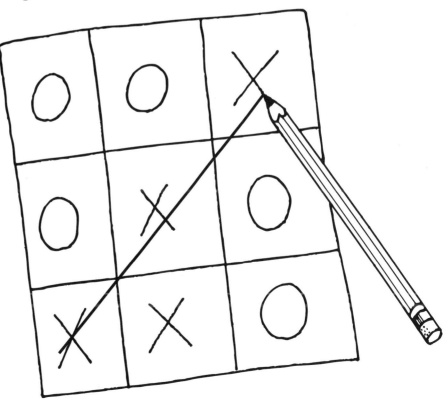

Name _____ Date _____

Fraction Speedway

How to Play: Take turns spinning the spinner and moving to the next equivalent fraction on the racetrack. If you choose an incorrect fraction, you must go back to your previous spot and miss a turn. The first player to reach the finish line wins.

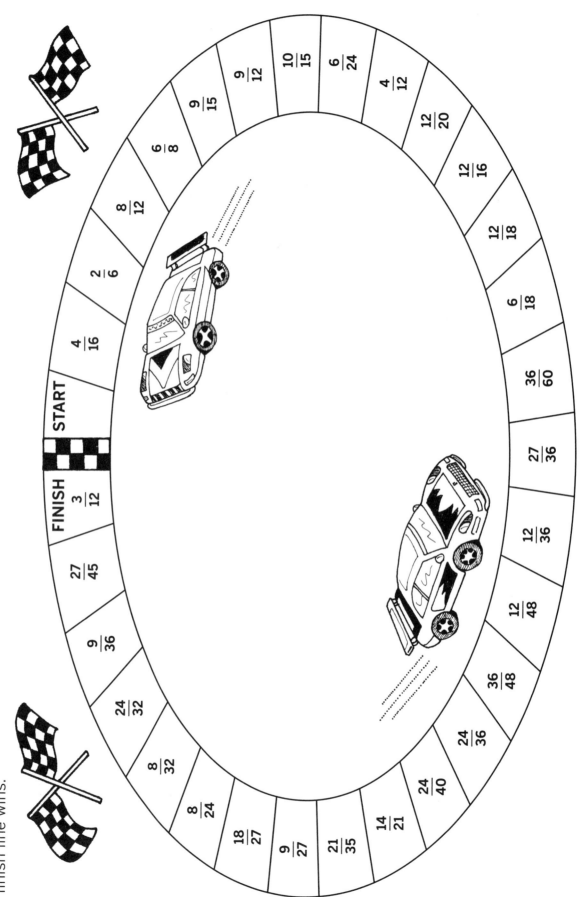

Fraction Tic-Tac-Toe

How to Play: Cut out the cards for one of the games and put them in a bag. Take turns drawing a card, solving the problem, and writing *X* or *O* on the answer in the Tic-Tac-Toe grid.

Game 1

$\frac{7}{18}$	$1\frac{13}{20}$	$1\frac{1}{12}$
$\frac{13}{28}$	$7\frac{5}{14}$	$6\frac{4}{15}$
$1\frac{3}{8}$	$5\frac{7}{12}$	$5\frac{15}{16}$

Game 2

$1\frac{1}{3}$	$1\frac{1}{6}$	$6\frac{2}{7}$
$5\frac{5}{6}$	$7\frac{2}{9}$	$1\frac{1}{2}$
$2\frac{1}{2}$	$1\frac{5}{7}$	$2\frac{1}{4}$

Game 3

$1\frac{11}{12}$	$1\frac{13}{16}$	$1\frac{11}{24}$
$1\frac{7}{15}$	$2\frac{1}{3}$	$\frac{2}{3}$
$2\frac{1}{2}$	$\frac{3}{5}$	$3\frac{2}{3}$

Game 1 $\frac{5}{9} - \frac{1}{6}$	**Game 1** $\frac{9}{10} + \frac{3}{4}$	**Game 1** $\frac{5}{6} + \frac{1}{4}$	**Game 1** $\frac{12}{15} - \frac{1}{5}$	**Game 1** $\frac{3}{4} - \frac{2}{7}$
Game 1 $1\frac{6}{7} + 5\frac{1}{2}$	**Game 1** $2\frac{3}{5} + 3\frac{2}{3}$	**Game 1** $5\frac{1}{8} - 3\frac{3}{4}$	**Game 1** $7\frac{3}{4} - 2\frac{1}{6}$	**Game 1** $3\frac{5}{16} + 2\frac{5}{8}$

Game 2 $1\frac{2}{3} \times \frac{4}{5}$	**Game 2** $\frac{1}{3} \times 3\frac{1}{2}$	**Game 2** $4\frac{2}{5} \times 1\frac{3}{7}$	**Game 2** $4\frac{1}{12} \times 1\frac{3}{7}$	**Game 2** $2\frac{1}{6} \times 3\frac{1}{3}$
Game 2 $4\frac{1}{3} \div 2\frac{8}{9}$	**Game 2** $4\frac{1}{6} \div 1\frac{2}{3}$	**Game 2** $9\frac{3}{7} \div 5\frac{1}{2}$	**Game 2** $5\frac{1}{4} \div 2\frac{1}{3}$	**Game 2** $2\frac{1}{7} \div 1\frac{2}{9}$

Game 3 $\frac{3}{4} + \frac{1}{3} + \frac{5}{6}$	**Game 3** $\frac{1}{4} + \frac{5}{8} + \frac{15}{16}$	**Game 3** $\frac{3}{8} + \frac{5}{6} + \frac{1}{4}$	**Game 3** $\frac{3}{5} + \frac{8}{15} + \frac{1}{3}$	**Game 3** $3\frac{2}{3} - \frac{5}{6} \div \frac{5}{8}$
Game 3 $\left(\frac{2}{3} + \frac{2}{5}\right) \div 1\frac{3}{5}$	**Game 3** $6 \div \frac{2}{3} \times \frac{5}{18}$	**Game 3** $\frac{1}{2} \div \frac{3}{4} \times \frac{9}{10}$	**Game 3** $2\frac{2}{9} \times \frac{3}{8} - \frac{1}{3}$	**Game 3** $6\frac{1}{3} - 3\frac{1}{3} \div 1\frac{1}{4}$

Spin to Win!

Materials

- Spinner reproducible
- overhead projector and transparency
- paper clips
- list of math terms and phrases
- "play" money (optional)
- colored pencils (optional)

Objective

Students will review math terminology while calculating a variety of money amounts.

This game is played similarly to the popular game show *Wheel of Fortune*® (a registered trademark of Califon Productions, Inc.). Players spin the wheel for money and guess the letters of a mystery phrase, earning the value of their spin for each correct letter. The mystery phrases are math terms that students use in their math class. This game gives students the opportunity to practice their math vocabulary as well as apply their calculating skills.

1. Use a copy of the Spinner reproducible (page 11) to make an overhead transparency of a money wheel to play Spin to Win! with the class. Divide the ten sections of the spinner into 20 sections and write a different amount of money in each section using either whole amounts or decimal values. Include two *Bankrupt* and two *Lose a Turn* sections. You might also include sections with percents of an amount, such as *25% of $350*.

2. Create a list of math phrases to use for the game, such as *Order of Operations, Greatest Common Factor, Prime Factorization,* and *Simplify and Solve.* Choose one of the phrases and write blank fill-in lines on the board for each letter of the phrase. Teams must take turns spinning the wheel for a money amount and calling out a letter to try to spell and guess the unknown phrase. The first team to guess the phrase correctly gets to keep their cumulative money earned during that round. Explain additional rules as follows:

   - Each team will earn the amount of money spun for each correct letter in the phrase. For example, if the mystery phrase is *Order of Operations*, and a team spins $350 and guesses the letter *r*, they earn 3 x $350 = $1,050 for the three *r*'s.
   - Players must pay $250 to call out a vowel and see if it is in the phrase.

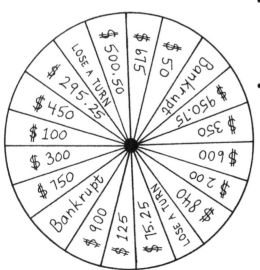

- If a team lands on *Bankrupt*, they lose all of their money accumulated from the current round, and the game continues with the next team taking a turn.
- If a team guesses a letter that is not in the phrase or a letter that has already been called, the game continues with the next team taking a turn.
- If a team incorrectly guesses the answer to the phrase, the game continues with the next team taking a turn.

3. Divide the class into teams and write team names on the board for scorekeeping. Explain how to play the game and show how to use a paper clip and pencil to spin the money wheel. Play a practice round with students to make sure they understand the rules of the game.

4. Create a "master letter list" by writing all the letters of the alphabet on the board. Have teams take turns spinning the wheel, guessing a letter, and calculating the money earned for each correct letter. After a team calls out a letter, cross it off the master list.

5. Have volunteers from each team keep track of their cumulative totals on the board. Encourage other team members to check and confirm those calculations.

6. The first team to correctly guess the phrase wins the money accumulated for that round. Play several rounds of the game using different phrases. The team with the most money at the end of the game (three or four rounds) wins.

7. After the game, discuss with the class the different strategies that they used to discover each phrase and obtain the largest amount of money with each spin.

Variation of the Game

Include "play" money, and have students count and make change during the game.

Math in the Mall

Materials
- Checks and Balance Sheet reproducible
- supplies to make board games

Objective
Students will apply a variety of "real life" math skills and strategies as they create and play a game about shopping in a mall.

This activity provides students with the opportunity to create their own board game, combining both their knowledge of math and their love of shopping.

1. Divide the class into pairs or small groups, and have them work cooperatively to create a board game about shopping at a mall. Give them the supplies that they need, or have them use their own, such as foam board, spinners or dice, newspaper and magazine cutouts of items for sale, index cards for game cards, play money, faux checks and credit cards, and play pieces to move around the game board. Encourage them to create a multi-dimensional game that includes a variety of math problems and involves several stores in the mall.

2. Require that students include these elements in their games:
   - Pictures or cutouts of priced items for sale, including items for both adults and children and for different parts of the home (e.g., kitchen, bedroom, bathroom)
   - Problem-solving cards about regular versus discounted items, credit cards versus cash purchases, sales tax, using coupons, and buying items on layaway
   - Checks to make purchases and balance sheets to record finances. Provide copies of the **Checks and Balance Sheet reproducible (page 33)**.
   - A complete set of game rules, including directions on how to play the game

3. Have students "spend a day in the mall" by playing each other's games. Monitor students as they play the games to make sure they are playing by the rules and performing correct calculations.

4. Afterwards, invite students to discuss which games worked the best, were the most fun to play, were the most challenging, and so on.

Name _____ Date _____

Checks and Balance Sheet

101

Date _____

Pay to the Order of _____ $ [   ]

_____ DOLLARS

Money Instructor Bank
1221 Main Street
Anywhere, USA 10001

For _____   _____

102

Date _____

Pay to the Order of _____ $ [   ]

_____ DOLLARS

Money Instructor Bank
1221 Main Street
Anywhere, USA 10001

For _____   _____

Check Number	Date	Check Paid To	Check/Deposit Amount	Balance

CHAPTER 2

Algebra

Value of the Variable

Objective

Students will model and solve algebraic equations using inverse operations to find the value of a variable.

For this game of hidden values, players write and solve algebraic equations to discover how many counters an opponent has hidden inside a bag. Students work with models to represent the value of variables.

Materials
- index cards
- balance scale
- counters
- paper lunch bags or envelopes
- cardboard dividers or file folders
- math journals or scratch paper

1. Write the following 16 equations (with their answers) on separate index cards. Create a set of 16 equation cards for each pair of students.

$x + 8 = 12$	$(x = 4)$	$3x + 3 = 12$	$(x = 3)$
$x + 5 = 10$	$(x = 5)$	$3x + 5 = 8$	$(x = 1)$
$2x + 4 = 12$	$(x = 4)$	$4x + 2 = 10$	$(x = 2)$
$5 + 2x = 11$	$(x = 3)$	$3 + 4x = 15$	$(x = 3)$
$2x + 7 = 15$	$(x = 4)$	$4x + 4 = 20$	$(x = 4)$
$10 + 2x = 14$	$(x = 2)$	$4x + 5 = 13$	$(x = 2)$
$3x + 6 = 21$	$(x = 5)$	$4 + 5x = 34$	$(x = 6)$
$7 + 3x = 13$	$(x = 2)$	$5x + 4 = 19$	$(x = 3)$

2. Introduce the game using a balance scale, counters, and paper bags to model how to solve for the variable in $2x + 7 = 15$.
   a. Secretly put four counters inside each of two paper bags (eight counters in all), and put the bags on the left side of the balance scale, along with seven more counters, to represent $2x + 7$. Place 15 counters on the right side of the scale.
   b. Write $2x + 7 = 15$ on the board, and explain to students that the balance scale is a model of that equation. It shows that both sides of the equation are equal.
   c. Go through the steps of isolating the variable to determine its value, pointing out that whatever is done to one side of the equation (scale) must also be done to the other side.
      - First, subtract 7 from both sides of the equation (scale), leaving $2x = 8$ counters. Remind students that subtraction is the inverse operation of addition.

Balanced Equation: $2x + 7 = 15$

- Next, divide both sides by 2 (remove one bag from the left side and four counters from the right side) to leave only x on the left and four counters on the right, or $x = 4$.

d. Prove algebraically that $x = 4$ by substituting 4 for x to show that $2(4) + 7 = 15$. Then open each bag to show the four counters inside (the value of x).

3. Tell students that they will play a game similar to what you modeled. Give each pair of students a cardboard divider (to block their opponent's view), a set of equation cards, counters, two equals ($=$) symbols written on separate index cards, and paper bags (or envelopes). Monitor students as they play, offering help as needed.

a. Players each choose an equation card from the stack. They use lunch bags, counters, and an equals symbol to secretly set up a model of their equation behind the cardboard divider, putting the same number of counters in each bag to represent the value of the variable x.

b. Players remove the divider to reveal their model. Opponents must write the equation modeled and solve for the variable to guess the number in each bag. If players solve the equation correctly, they earn points equal to the value of the variable for that equation. For example, if $x = 5$, players earn five points. If players do not solve the equation correctly, they place the card back on the stack. If players set up an equation incorrectly, they lose one point.

c. The player with the most points at the end of the game wins.

Variation of the Game

Include both positive and negative numbers, using green counters for positive numbers and red counters for negative numbers. Players "cancel out the red" (negative numbers) by adding the same number of green counters. For example, using the equation $2x - 4 = 8$, model -4 with four red counters and then cancel out -4 from the left side of the equation by adding four green counters to both sides to show $2x = 12$.

Color Wheel Race

Materials
- Color Wheel Race reproducible
- index cards
- paper lunch bags
- math journals or scratch paper
- crayons or colored pencils

Objective

Students will solve one-step equations with decimals to find the value of a variable.

In this game, players race to identify and color circles on a number wheel that show answers corresponding to variables of chosen algebraic equations.

1. Write the following 16 equations and answers on separate index cards. Create one set of 32 cards for each pair of students.

Equations	Answers
$a + 1.8 = 4.4$	6.6
$h - 0.5 = 9.9$	2.9
$5.9 + k = 6.7$	0.8
$n + 1.819 = 6.619$	2.6
$15.1 - r = 8.5$	10.4
$t - 2.5 = 0.4$	6.9
$10.2 - v = 3.3$	4.8
$8.1 + w = 14.5$	6.4
$x + 4.3 = 5.5$	1.2
$y - 1.4 = 0.9$	2.3
$12.1 - g = 9.0$	0.9
$5.6 - f = 2.8$	3.6
$b + 12.5 = 13.4$	1.7
$c - 1.9 = 1.7$	0.4
$7.8 + p = 9.5$	3.1
$e + 10.6 = 11.0$	2.8

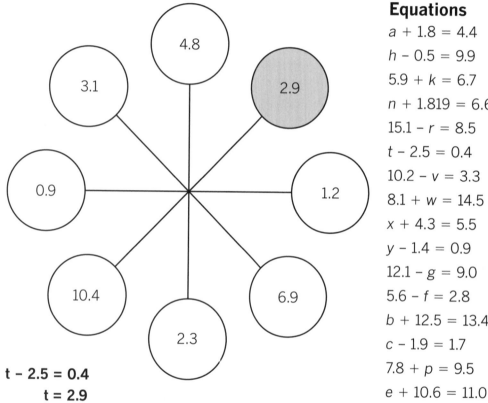

$t - 2.5 = 0.4$
$t = 2.9$

2. Give each pair of students a copy of the **Color Wheel Race reproducible (page 38)**, a set of equation cards, a set of answer cards, and a paper bag. Read the directions aloud, and demonstrate how to play the game. (If needed, review how to solve for a variable.)

   a. Players place the equation cards in a bag and distribute the answer cards equally.

   b. Players write their eight answers in the circles of their wheel, one answer per circle.

c. Players race against their opponent, drawing equation cards one at a time, solving for the variable, and looking for that answer in their wheel. If the answer is there, players color that circle; if not, they have to put the card back into the bag. The first player to finish coloring his or her wheel wins.

3. Tell students to write their answers in dark print and color the circles lightly so the answers can still be seen.

4. Monitor students as they play the game and check their work for accuracy. Consider having students solve each equation in their math journal and then write the letter of the variable next to its corresponding answer in their wheel (e.g., $t = 2.9$).

5. Invite students to play again using Wheels 3 and 4 on the Color Wheel reproducible.

Variations of the Game

• Challenge students to use multi-step equations (and answers) that you have listed on the board instead of using the equations and answers provided.

• Students may play the game on their own, racing against the clock as follows:
   a. Find four pairs of answer cards that add up to four, and write those answers in connected pairs of circles in Wheel 1.
   b. Arrange the remaining answer cards into pairs that have a difference of four, and write those answers in connected pairs of circles in Wheel 2.
   c. Solve each equation and write the variable next to its answer in the wheel.

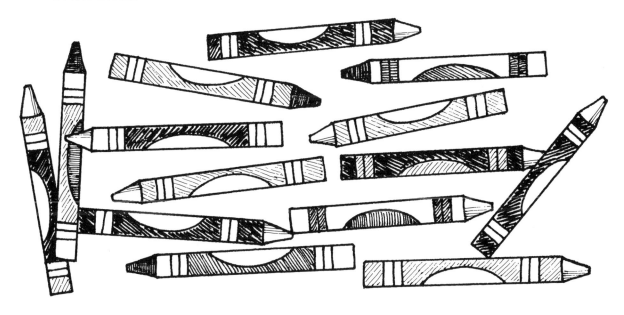

Algebra **37**

Color Wheel Race

How to Play:

1. Place the equation cards in a bag and distribute the answer cards equally.

2. Write your eight answers in the circles of your wheel, one answer per circle.

3. Race against your opponent to draw equation cards one at a time, solve for the variable, and look for that answer in your wheel. If the answer is there, color that circle; if not, put the card back. The first player to finish coloring his or her wheel wins.

Wheel 1
Player: _____

Wheel 2
Player: _____

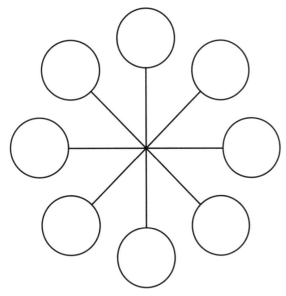
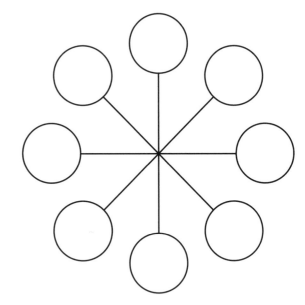

Wheel 3
Player: _____

Wheel 4
Player: _____

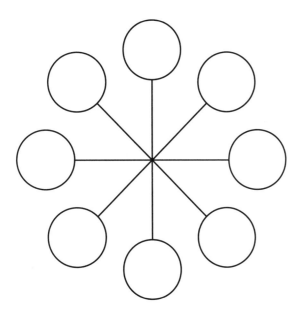
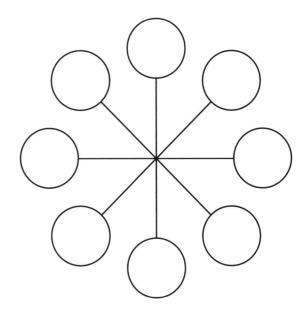

Capture the Spy

Objective

Students will solve multi-step algebraic equations to find the value of a variable.

In this exciting game of pursuit, players try to avoid capture by solving equations that allow them to move to different places on a game board. They must use their knowledge of algebra and some strategic planning to outsmart their opponent.

Materials
- Capture the Spy Game Board reproducible
- overhead transparency and projector
- index cards
- two colors of counters
- math journals or scratch paper

1. Before the game, write the following equations on the board. Invite each pair of students to copy the equations onto index cards, one equation per card. These will be the game cards. You might also write other equations on the board for students to use. (Note that the value of each x should be from zero to six.)

$$-5x + 8 = -7 \qquad\qquad -2(6 + x) - x = -18$$
$$4x - 3 = 1 \qquad\qquad 9(x + 3) - 3x = 39$$
$$9x + 3 = 48 \qquad\qquad 5(x - 6) + 3x = -6$$
$$6 + x/5 = 7 \qquad\qquad -10 = -4 - x$$
$$14 = 2 + 3x \qquad\qquad 13x - 21 = 44$$
$$-3x + 5 = 5 \qquad\qquad 8x + 22 = 70$$
$$-35 = (3 + x)(-5) \qquad\qquad (4/5)x = 3(1/5)$$
$$3x + 2(x - 6) = -2 \qquad\qquad (3/8)x = 3/4$$
$$-4(x - 3) = 8 \qquad\qquad 3/x = 81/135$$

2. Place a transparency of the **Capture the Spy Game Board reproducible (page 41)** on the overhead projector, and use it to explain and demonstrate how to play the game.

3. Give each student pair a Capture the Spy Game Board reproducible. Encourage students to check each other's work as they play the game, making sure they are solving for the value of x correctly and moving that number of spaces. Point out that if a player solves for x incorrectly, he or she loses a turn.

How to Play Capture the Spy:

a. One player is the "Spy," using only one counter on the game board. The other player moves all the "Agents," which are three counters of another color.

b. The three Agents start on the two circles with the small magnifying glass and the *W* (only one counter per circle). The Spy starts on any unoccupied circle except the one between the two small magnifying glasses.

c. The goal of the Agents is to capture the Spy by either landing on the same space or cornering the Spy on the *L* circle (*Lose*). The goal of the Spy is to keep away from the Agents and land exactly on the *W* circle (*Win*).

d. Starting with the Agents, players take turns choosing a game card and solving for *x* to determine how many spaces they move their counter. (Only one Agent can be moved per turn.) Players must move that exact number or they lose their turn.

e. An Agent can move only left, right, or up to any unoccupied circle connected by a line. (All Agents must be moved.) The Spy can move in any direction (up, down, left, right, diagonal, and backward) to any unoccupied circle connected by a line.

f. The game continues until the Spy is captured or the Spy lands on the *W* circle. If all the game cards are used before there is a winner, shuffle and reuse them.

4. Monitor students as they play the game, offering assistance as needed. Encourage them to solve each equation on scratch paper or in their math journal.

5. After the game, have students discuss different playing strategies.

Variation of the Game

Invite students to think of other variations of the game that they could play. For example, they could draw their own game board or use polynomials for the cards.

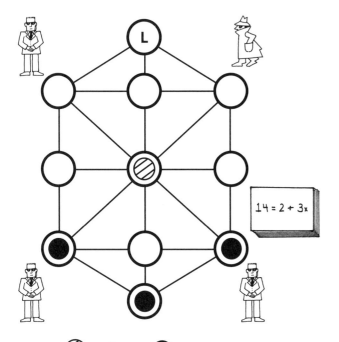

$14 = 2 + 3x$

⊘ = Spy ● = Agents

Capture the Spy Game Board

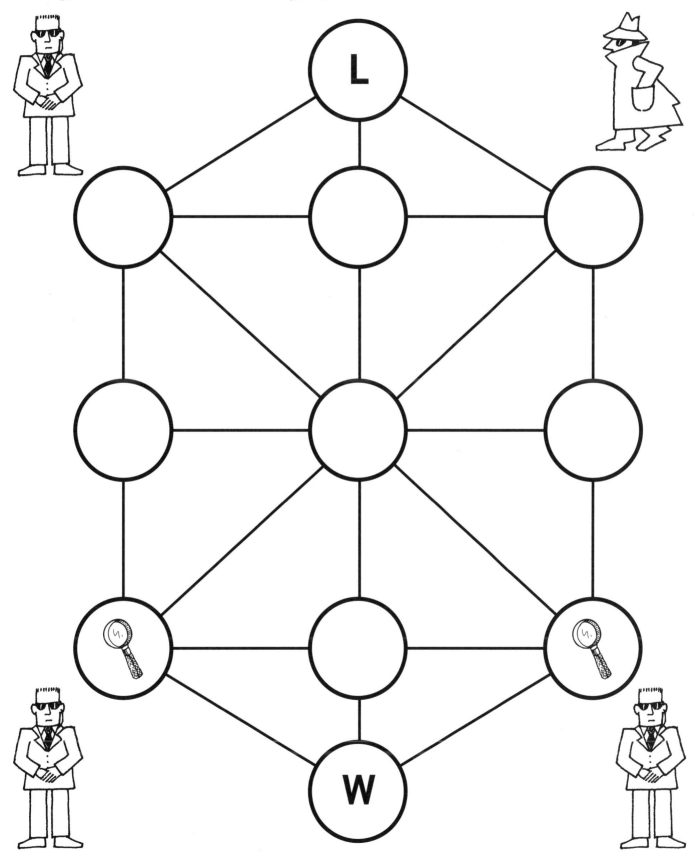

Outdoor Algebra

Materials

- orange cones (or other relay markers)
- numeral and symbol cards (0–9, +, –, ×, ÷, x, y, | |, •, /)
- algebraic equations written on index cards
- scratch paper for scorekeeping and problem solving
- plastic toy eggs and egg cartons (optional)
- plastic spoons (optional)

Objective

Students will solve a variety of algebraic equations involving variables, combining like terms, and using absolute value.

The following games are a great way to practice math on a sunny day. You may use a variety of algebraic equations for the games, such as two-step and three-step equations with variables on one or both sides, combining like terms, and using absolute value. For a greater challenge, include equations and word problems that involve multiplication and division of integers, fractions, decimals, and exponents.

Algebra Relay

1. Divide the class into two or three teams. Spread out four cones on a playing field for each team, so students can weave through them as they relay back and forth from one end to the other. At the end of each setup, spread out two sets of numeral and symbol cards for each team to use for the relay.

2. Tell students that the goal of the relay is for teams to build and solve algebraic equations that you say aloud. Each team lines up and sends one player at a time to get the numeral and symbol cards needed to build the equation. Players may take only one card at a time and must weave through the cones to and from the cards. (If they skip a cone or grab the wrong card, they must start over.)

3. Players then tag the next teammate to continue the relay. After building the equation, they solve for the variable. The first team to do so correctly earns two points. The other teams will earn one point if they build and solve the equation correctly.

4. Play several rounds of the game using different equations, such as those with two steps ($3x - 12 = 27$), variables on both sides ($24x + 38 = -14x$), and absolute value ($3 - |x - 5| = -2$). The team with the most points wins.

$$\boxed{3}\ \boxed{X}\ \boxed{-}\ \boxed{1}\ \boxed{2}\ \boxed{=}\ \boxed{2}\ \boxed{7}$$

Variation of the Game

Play the game using plastic eggs instead of cards. Label the eggs with individual digits and symbols. Teammates use a spoon to carry eggs that are part of the given equation, without dropping them (or else start over). They will build the equation in an egg carton at the opposite end of the field. After teams complete the equation, they solve for the variable.

978-1-4129-5926-1

Algebra Fitness

1. Prepare four identical sets of algebraic equation cards (one equation per card) that include only one variable, such as $5x + 13 = 38$. Prepare the same number of exercise cards, one type of exercise per card, such as: *Do _____ sit-ups.*

2. Divide the class into four teams, and have each team line up at a starting line. Place the equation cards and exercise cards at the opposite end of the field. Shuffle the cards in each stack so each team starts with a different problem.

3. When you say *go,* the first person from each team races to pick up both an equation card and an exercise card. The player then returns to his or her team, where everyone solves the equation for the variable. After they tell you the correct answer, the team then performs that many repetitions of the chosen exercise. For example, for $5x + 13 = 38$ ($x = 5$), the team does five sit-ups. If the exercise involves a partner (such as sit-ups), teammates must trade off so each player does the required repetitions.

4. The game continues until all the cards are used. The first team to finish wins.

Variation of the Game

Include both positive and negative answers, with girls on each team doing the exercises for positive answers and boys doing them for negative answers.

Materials
- algebraic equations written on index cards
- exercises written on index cards
- scratch paper or math journals for problem solving

$5x + 13 = 38$; $x = 5$ sit-ups

Polynomial Shuffle

Objective
Students will create and solve polynomial equations.

In this game, students create and solve polynomial equations as they play a mathematical version of shuffleboard. They slide their "pucks" onto a game board of algebraic terms, trying to build an equation with the greatest possible solution.

1. Use the **Shuffleboard reproducible (page 46)** to set up a game of shuffleboard for each pair of students. Label the seven sections
   of each game board from top to bottom x^2, $2x$, $4x$, 3, 6, $-x$, -1. Make two enlarged paper (or chalk-drawn) versions for Floor Shuffleboard or one regular copy for Tabletop Shuffleboard, as follows:

   Floor Shuffleboard: Make ten "pucks" by placing uncooked rice between two paper plates and securely taping the edges of the plates together. Make five of one color for Player 1 and five of a different color for Player 2. Tape two large Shuffleboard game boards at opposite ends of a long strip of butcher paper (at least five feet long), with their apexes (points) facing inward. Players stand at opposite ends of the butcher paper and use yardsticks (or other long sticks) to slide their pucks onto the game board at the opposite end.

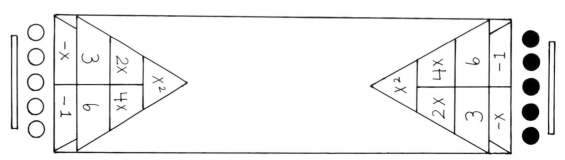

   Tabletop Shuffleboard: Each player uses five counters (or coins) for their pucks and take turns sliding their pucks onto the same Shuffleboard game board taped to the opposite end of a long table. Players may use their pencil or thumb to push each counter.

2. Players take turns sliding each of their five pucks onto the game board to score points. Each puck scores only if it lies entirely within a section, not touching any boundary lines. (Players may not repeat their turn.) A player may also knock out an opponent's puck, eliminating that score from the round.

Materials
- Shuffleboard reproducible
- butcher paper
- small paper plates (2 different colors)
- uncooked rice
- tape
- yardsticks or any long sticks
- circular counters or coins
- dice
- math journals or scratch paper for scorekeeping

3. Players record their scores by adding like terms. They earn a "double score" if they can form a factorable polynomial; for example, $x^2 + 6x + 9$, which can be factored as $(x + 3)(x + 3)$.

4. Players then roll a die to determine the value of x, which they substitute into their equation to calculate the points earned. For example, if they roll a three and their equation is $x^2 + 2x + 8$, then they earn $(3)^2 + 2(3) + 8 = 23$ points. The player with the most points after five rounds wins.

5. Circulate around the class and monitor students' progress as they play the game. Encourage them to check each other's calculations to confirm the points earned.

Variation of the Game

Set up a series of Shuffleboard games outdoors by using different values in each pair of triangles. Have students compete in a whole-class Shuffleboard Tournament.

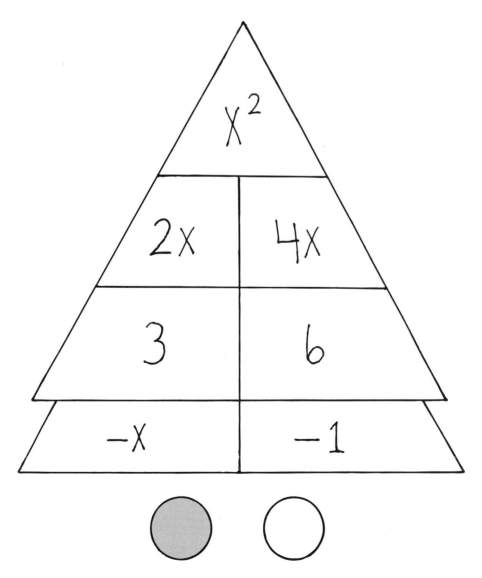

Shuffleboard

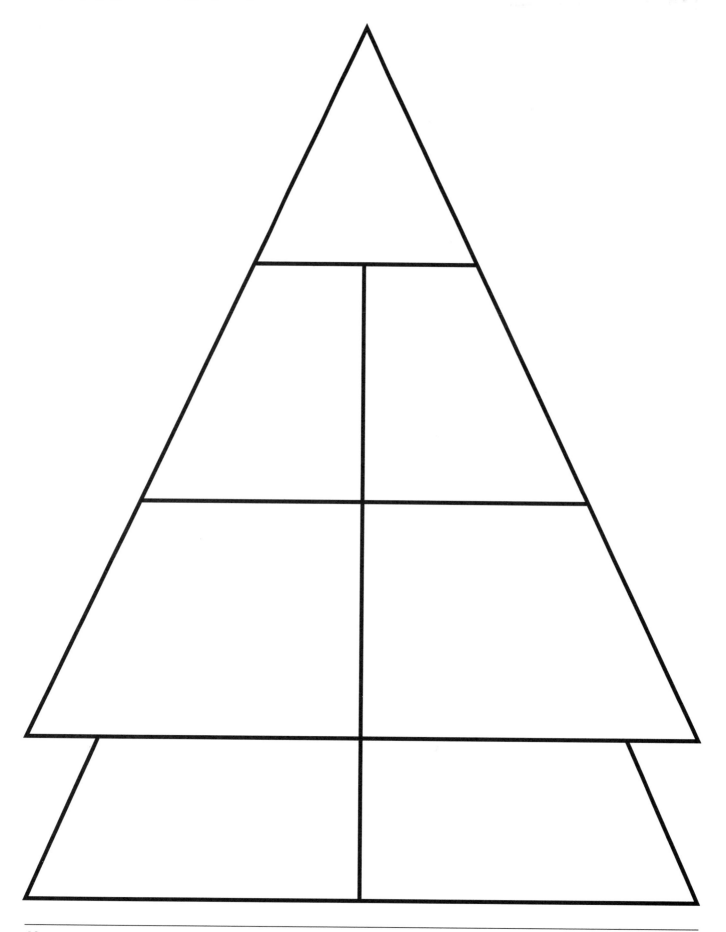

Algebraic Scramble

Objective

Students will use numeral and symbol tiles to display and solve algebraic equations.

This algebraic activity is played similarly to the popular game *Scrabble*® (a registered trademark of Hasbro, Inc.). In this version of the game, players must assemble and solve mathematical equations.

1. Set up each game by using six sheets of the **Inch Grid Paper reproducible (page 49)**—two for the game board (taped together), two for the "number tiles," and two for the "symbol tiles." For the number tiles, write *0–9* repetitively (one numeral per square) to fill the page. You might also choose to include fractions and exponents. For the symbol tiles, make one row each of the symbols +, −, ×, ÷, =, ( ), and two rows of *y* tiles (for the variable). Copy the set of six pages onto cardstock to make a set for each group of players.

2. Give each group of two to four players a game board and sheets of number and symbol tiles to cut apart and store in two separate resealable bags (one bag for the number tiles and one bag for the symbol tiles). Do not cut apart the squares on the game board.

3. Give each group the **Algebraic Scramble Rules reproducible (page 48)** and review the rules with students. Use an overhead projector to explain and demonstrate how to play the game. Check for understanding before having students play on their own.

4. Monitor students as they play the game. Check that they are solving for the variable correctly and are using the game tiles as directed. Remind students that the subtraction symbol may also be used as a negative sign. Students might also use the *x* symbol as either a multiplication sign or the variable *x*.

Materials
- Algebraic Scramble Rules reproducible
- Inch Grid Paper reproducible
- cardstock
- scissors
- tape
- resealable plastic bags
- overhead projector and transparencies
- cardboard dividers (strips of 4" x 10" cardboard, folded in half lengthwise)

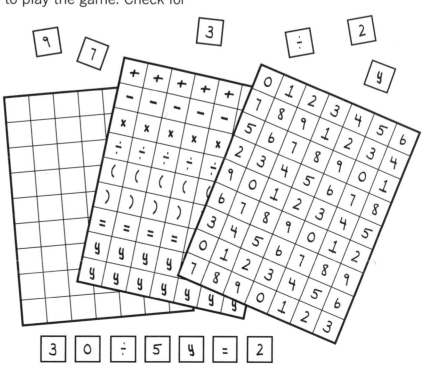

Algebraic Scramble Rules

How to Play

1. Players start by each taking nine number tiles and nine symbol tiles from the bags and placing them behind their cardboard divider, away from their opponents' view.

2. The first player places a correct equation in the center of the board, one tile per square, either vertically or horizontally. The equation may not include greater than a two-digit number.

   a. For an equation with no variables, the player earns the points equal to the answer of that equation. For an equation with a variable, he or she earns the points equal to double or triple the value of the variable—double for one-step equations and triple for multiple-step equations.

   For example:
   - $3 \times 4 = 12$, the player gets 12 points.
   - $4y = 36$, the value of $y = 9$, so the player gets $2 \times 9 = 18$ points.
   - $2y + 5 = 25$, the value of $y = 10$, so the player gets $3 \times 10 = 30$ points.

   b. Players choose another tile from one of the bags for every tile that they use.

   c. If players do not have any tiles that form a correct equation, they may use their turn to exchange up to four tiles, and then wait until their next turn to use them.

   d. If players show an incorrect equation, they lose five points and must wait until their next turn to try again. If a player incorrectly challenges an opponent's equation, he or she loses five points.

3. The game continues with players taking turns building math equations using one of the tiles already placed on the board (without moving that tile) and other tiles that they selected from the bags. Equations can be only vertical and horizontal, not diagonal.

4. Players record their cumulative points. The player with the most points at the end of the game wins.

Inch Grid Paper

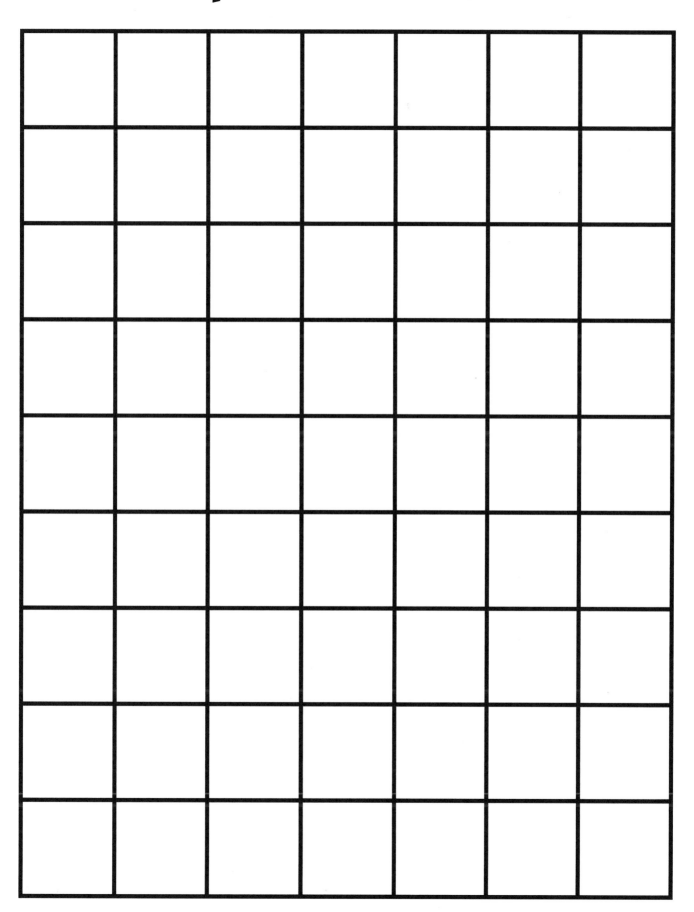

CHAPTER 3

Geometry

Polygon Jumble

Objective

Students will identify and classify polygons according to specific characteristics.

This game is played similarly to the popular commercial game *Twister®* (a registered trademark of Hasbro, Inc.). In this whole-class kinesthetic game of Polygon Jumble, students use their hands and feet to touch geometric shapes corresponding to descriptions on a spinner. The goal of the game is to stretch and touch each described shape without falling over!

Materials
- Spinner reproducible
- paper clips
- overhead transparency and projector (optional)
- floor mat or butcher paper
- thick black marker
- construction paper
- scissors
- tape

1. Use a copy of the Spinner reproducible (page 11) to make a spinner that has descriptions of five different polygons (two sections per polygon). For example: *A three-sided polygon with all equal sides.* You may use different kinds of polygons or just one category of polygons (e.g., triangles). Make another spinner labeled *Left Hand, Right Hand, Left Foot, Right Foot* (two sections each). For the last two sections, write *Either Hand* and *Either Foot.* (If you prefer, you may make spinners to use on an overhead projector.)

2. Cut out six paper shapes from construction paper for each polygon on the spinner (30 shapes in all). You may use either congruent or similar shapes for each polygon. Draw a large 5 x 6 grid on a floor mat or large sheet of butcher paper. Tape a shape in each square to create a large walk-on game mat. Create a game mat for each group of three to five players, or have groups take turns playing on a classroom mat.

3. Explain the rules to students. Invite volunteers to demonstrate how to play the game. Check for understanding before having students play on their own.

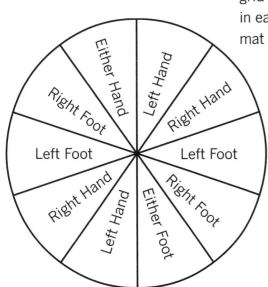

a. To play the game, spin both spinners and read aloud the descriptions. Students must put their hand or foot (left or right) on top of one of the correct shapes on the game mat. They may not use the same shape as another player, and they cannot move their hand or foot once they place it on a shape.

b. Continue spinning the spinners and reading the descriptions. Players move their hand or foot to the next correct shape, without moving the other hand or foot from its place. If players put their hand or foot on the wrong shape or they lose their balance and fall over, they are out of the game. The last player on the mat wins!

4. Play several games in order to reinforce the mathematical concepts involved in the game.

Variations of the Game

Create different game mats and spinners (or have students create them), and then have groups rotate to play the different versions. For example:

- triangles (equilateral acute, isosceles acute, isosceles obtuse, isosceles right, scalene acute, scalene obtuse, scalene right)

- quadrilaterals (parallelogram, rectangle, rhombus, square, trapezoid)

- angles (supplementary, complementary, vertical, alternate interior, alternate exterior, corresponding, consecutive interior, consecutive exterior)

- solid figures (sphere, cylinder, cone, different kinds of prisms and pyramids)

Gin Rummy Geometry

Materials
- Gin Rummy Geometry Rules reproducible
- unlined index cards
- protractors
- rulers

Objective
Students will draw, identify, and sort geometric figures.

In this version of the card game *Gin Rummy,* students will sort and classify geometric shapes according to common attributes. You will need two class sessions for this game, one for making the cards and one for playing the game.

1. Give each pair of students 54 unlined index cards to create a deck of Gin Rummy Geometry cards. Have them draw and label three examples each of the following geometric figures (one per card), including the measures of interior angles and nick-marks showing congruent sides and angles:

 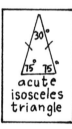 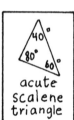

acute equilateral triangle	quadrilateral (square)
acute isosceles triangle	quadrilateral (trapezoid)
acute scalene triangle	pentagon
right isosceles triangle	hexagon
right scalene triangle	heptagon
obtuse isosceles triangle	octagon
obtuse scalene triangle	decagon
quadrilateral (parallelogram)	any solid figure
quadrilateral (rectangle)	(e.g., prisms, pyramids)
quadrilateral (rhombus)	

2. Give students a copy of the **Gin Rummy Geometry Rules reproducible (page 53)**, and review the rules. Then demonstrate how to play the game. Invite volunteers to help you show each step of the game. Check for understanding before students play on their own.

3. Monitor students as they play the game. You might have them rotate partners or trade cards so they have the opportunity to play with other students and geometric figures.

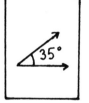 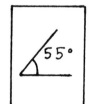 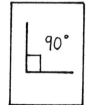

Variation of the Game
Instead of using polygons and solid figures, players may use angles from 0° to 270°, at increments of 5°. They can play the game by sorting the cards into congruent angles, complementary angles (sum of 90°), supplementary angles (sum of 180°), or a series of sequential angles.

Gin Rummy Geometry Rules

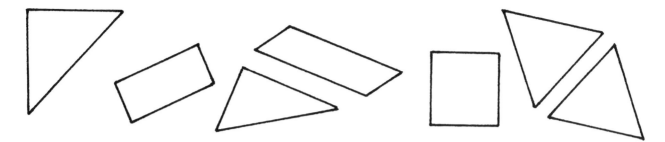

Object of the Game:

The object of the game is to collect and sort all of your cards into "sets" or "sequences" of three or more shapes without any cards left over.

A **set** has the same type of shape (e.g., three acute triangles, three acute equilateral triangles), whereas a **sequence** has a series of shapes with an increasing number of angles (e.g., three angles of a triangle, four angles of a quadrilateral, five angles of a pentagon). Each card can be used in only one group at a time (no overlapping).

How to Play:

1. Deal ten cards to each player. Players keep their cards in their hands at all times, away from their opponents' view. Turn the top card of the deck faceup to start the discard pile. Place the rest of the deck facedown in a stockpile.

2. Players take turns selecting one card from either the top of the discard pile, which is faceup for all to see, or from the top of the stockpile, which is facedown. To complete their turn, players must discard one card from their hand and place it faceup on the discard pile. Note that if the top card from the discard pile is taken, the player must discard a *different* card that same turn.

3. The game ends when a player calls out *Gin Rummy Geometry*, puts down all of his or her cards to show complete sets or sequences, and discards a card on the stockpile. If the stockpile is used up before a winner is declared, shuffle and reuse the discard pile.

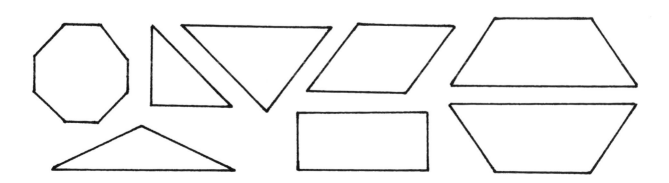

Puzzling Pentominoes

Materials

- Pentominoes reproducible
- Inch Grid Paper reproducible
- scissors
- colored pencils

Objective

Students will use the transformation of geometric puzzle pieces to cover rectangles of different sizes.

In this game, students use the transformation of pentominoes (five-square figures) to complete rectangular shapes. Players must use both visual perception and spatial reasoning to finish their pentominoes puzzles first.

1. Explain to students that *pentominoes* are plane figures made of exactly five connected congruent squares with at least one shared side. There are 12 different pentominoes. Each pentomino is unique so it cannot be transformed (rotated, reflected, or translated) to match any of the other pentominoes.

2. Give students a copy of the **Pentominoes reproducible (page 56)** to color and cut apart, or have them use Inch Grid Paper reproducible (page 49) to draw, color, and cut out their own set of the 12 different pentominoes. Have students identify which pentominoes have reflective symmetry and which ones do not.

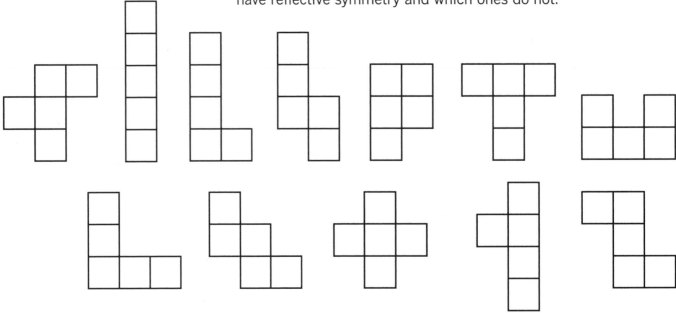

3. Explain that pentominoes can be put together like puzzle pieces to form different shapes. Show an example. Explain that the goal of the game is to be the first player to find an arrangement of pentominoes that covers a given rectangle. The rectangle can be 3 x 5 (using three pentominoes), 4 x 5 (using four pentominoes), or 6 x 10 (using all 12 pentominoes). Players may use any orientation of pentominoes without gaps or overlaps.

4. Divide the class into pairs, and have each student cut out a 3 x 5 rectangle, a 4 x 5 rectangle, and a 6 x 10 rectangle from one-inch grid paper. Have pairs compete against each other to see who can complete each rectangle first. Players may take turns choosing one of their pentominoes to put in their rectangle or rearrange an existing one (one move per turn), or they can race against each other (or a timer) to complete their entire rectangle.

5. Invite students to share different solutions for each rectangle. (Note that there are many possible solutions.) You might also challenge them to identify any solutions that are *isomorphic*—can be flipped or rotated to look exactly the same.

Variations of the Game

- Have students draw a rectangle (or other shape) with an area of 60 squares and cover it using all 12 pentominoes without any gaps or overlaps.

- Point out that many different shapes can be created using the same 12 pentominoes simply by sliding, rotating, and flipping pentominoes. Invite students to explore and display different shapes using some or all of their pentominoes.

- Have students draw and cut out five different *tetrominoes* (four connected squares). Then ask them to work with a partner and use both tetromino sets to cover rectangles of 40 squares.

- Give students plastic or wood *tangram* pieces, another puzzle of geometric shapes that consists of seven different polygons (two small congruent triangles, two large congruent triangles, one medium-sized triangle, one small square, and one parallelogram). All the tangrams fit together to form a large square. Have students compare pentominoes to tangrams. They may race to put together one or two sets of tangrams to form a large square. Encourage students to make other figures with the tangram pieces and then measure and compare the area of each shape.

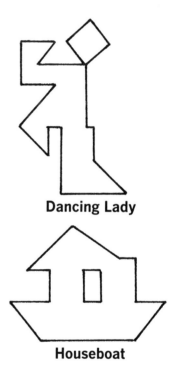

Dancing Lady

Houseboat

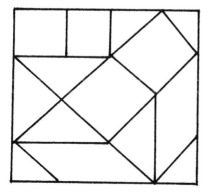

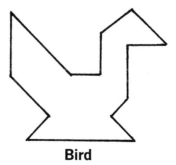

Bird

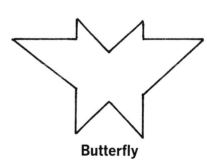

Butterfly

Name _____   Date _____

Pentominoes

Directions: Color within the bold lines and cut apart the pentominoes to play the game.

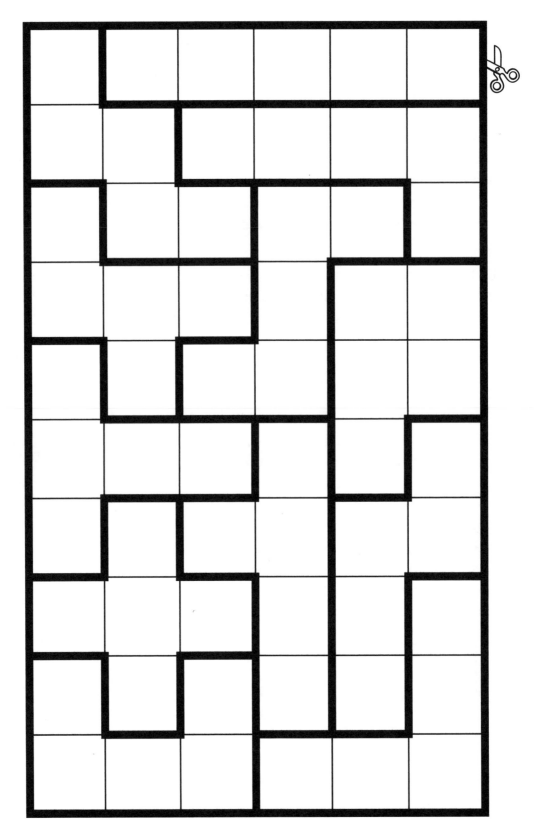

Cover Up

Objective

Students will draw and calculate the area of polygons in order to fill a given region.

In this game, students decide how to use triangular units of measure to draw different polygons that will cover up the greatest area. By using both spatial reasoning and formulas for area, players decide the best way to draw each shape.

1. Give each group of two or three students a copy of the **Triangular Grid Paper reproducible (page 59)**, two copies of the Spinner reproducible (page 11), two paper clips, and colored pencils. Review how to make the spinners, having students label the sections of one spinner *2–11* and the other spinner with names of the following five polygons (two sections each): *triangle, parallelogram, trapezoid, pentagon, hexagon.*

2. Tell students that the triangular grid paper is made of equilateral triangles with one-centimeter sides. Explain that they will be using the grid paper to draw different polygons and calculate their area using formulas: triangle = $1/2bh$, parallelogram = bh, trapezoid = $1/2 h(b_1 + b_2)$.

3. Also review how to divide an equilateral triangle into two right triangles and use the Pythagorean Theorem ($a^2 + b^2 = c^2$; where a = height, b = base, c = hypotenuse) to calculate the length of its height (a).

4. Explain that the goal is to color and cover up the greatest possible area of the triangular grid paper. Then explain and demonstrate how to play the game:
   a. Players take turns spinning both spinners. The first spin determines which polygon they will draw. The second spin determines how many total triangular units they can use to draw one or more of those polygons in any orientation, depending on the space available. For example, if they spin *trapezoid* and *11,* they can draw two trapezoids, one with eight triangular units and one with three triangular units. Students must determine which combination will equal the spun area, *11.*
   b. After players color their polygon(s), they must use the appropriate formula to calculate and record the area in square centimeters.

    c. Players continue taking turns spinning the spinners, coloring the shapes, and calculating the area. When the grid paper is completely colored (or when time is up), the player with the greatest total area colored wins.

5. Monitor students' progress and remind them to check each other's calculations throughout the game.

6. After the game, invite students to cut out and compare the shapes they drew. They can identify congruent and similar polygons, symmetrical polygons (rotational or reflective symmetry), and those with the same perimeter or area.

Variation of the Game

For a simpler version of the game, have players use either regular centimeter or one-inch grid paper and shade in only rectangular shapes of the grid. Players can spin the number spinner twice to determine the length and width of the area to color. They may also use one-inch color tiles to cover areas of the grid.

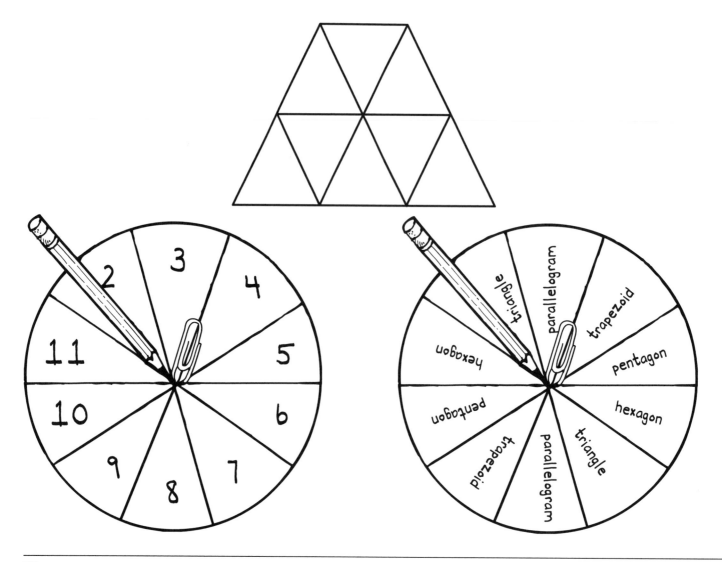

Triangular Grid Paper

Fill 'Er Up!

Materials

- Fill 'Er Up! Nets reproducible
- sets of rectangular gift boxes
- cardstock
- scissors
- tape

Objective

Students will build and determine the volume of different solid figures.

In this game, teams race to build different solid-figure building blocks to fill up rectangular containers. They must use teamwork and their knowledge of volume to decide which combination of blocks will fill up their container the quickest.

1. Divide the class into teams, and give each team an identical gift box, a supply of the **Fill 'Er Up! Nets reproducible (page 61)** copied onto cardstock, scissors, and tape.

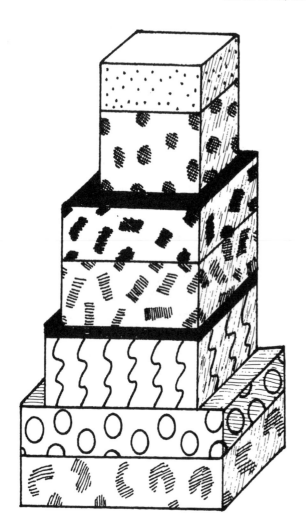

2. Explain that the goal of the game is to be the first team to fill up their gift box with the correct number of "building blocks." They will determine the number of blocks using the volume of the box and the dimension of each block. (The blocks must be stacked, not placed randomly.) Teams must build the blocks they use from those on the reproducible: cubes, rectangular prisms, and one-inch or two-inch triangular prisms. Teams must decide which blocks to use, how many they need to make, and how to work together to get the job done.

3. Circulate around the room to monitor teams' progress as they race to fill up their gift box. Suggest that they show their calculations on paper to prove their work. You might also display a list of formulas for volume that students can refer to during the game: cube = s^3, rectangular prism = lwh, triangular prism = $1/2lwh$.

4. Play several rounds of the game, having teams fill a different-sized box for each round. After several rounds, invite students to discuss the strategies they used.

Variations of the Game

- Set a limit for the number of cubic blocks that can be used (e.g., ten cubes), requiring teams to use a variety of figures.

- For a simpler game, have students use only cubic blocks. You might also provide one-inch connecting cubes or wooden cubes.

Fill 'Er Up! Nets

Cube

One-inch Triangular Prism

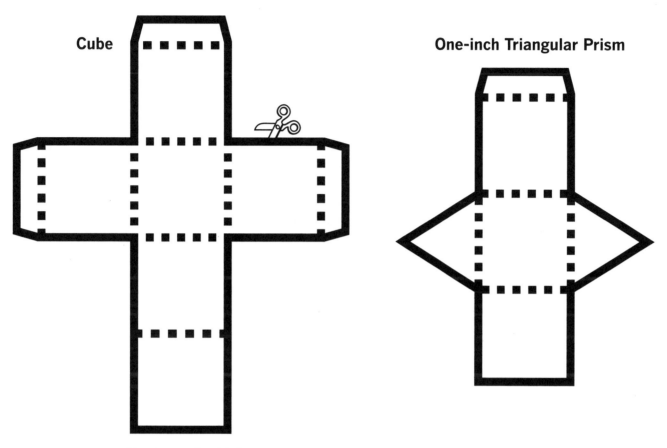

Rectangular Prism

Two-inch Triangular Prism

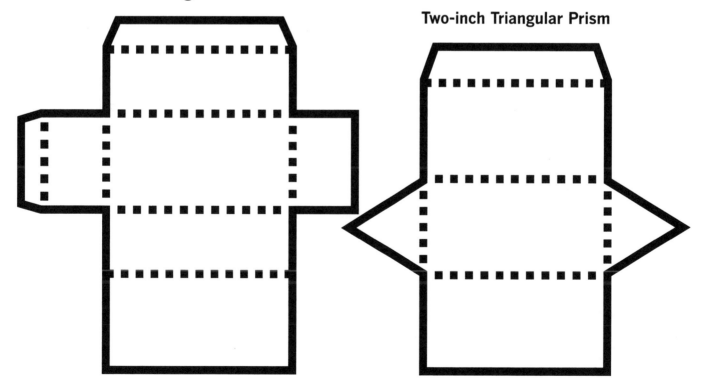

Coordinate Battle-Shapes

Materials
- Coordinate Battle-Shapes reproducible
- overhead projector and transparency
- cardboard dividers or file folders
- colored pencils
- protractors or rulers

Objective
Students will identify ordered pairs used to plot geometric shapes on a coordinate grid.

This geometric coordinates game is played similarly to the popular commercial game *Battleship*® (a registered trademark of Hasbro, Inc.), in which players call out ordered pairs in an effort to locate their opponent's hidden fleet of "battle-shapes" plotted on a coordinate grid. Players keep track of their own and their opponent's hits as they try to be the first to "capture" the shapes.

1. Ask students to find a partner, and give each student two copies of the **Coordinate Battle-Shapes reproducible (page 64)**, a cardboard divider to block their opponent's view, colored pencils, and a protractor. Use an overhead projector and a transparency to review how to plot ordered pairs in the four quadrants of a coordinate grid, connecting the points to show a polygon.

2. Explain that the goal of Coordinate Battle-Shapes is to use ordered pairs to try to locate all of an opponent's hidden fleet of "battle-shapes." Demonstrate how to play the game as follows:

   a. Players (student pairs) sit across from or next to each other with a cardboard divider between them to block each other's view. Each player gets two copies of the Coordinate Battle-Shapes reproducible, one to draw their own shapes and the other to show the "hits" and "misses" in locating their opponent's shapes. They place the papers side by side, titling one *My Shapes* and the other *My Opponent's Shapes*.

   b. Each player secretly draws his or her own set of four geometric shapes in different locations on the grid. The shapes may be either polygons or solid figures (whichever players decide), and they must be at least one inch high, one inch wide, and cannot touch each other. All the vertices of the shapes must also be drawn at intersection points of the gridlines (not in between lines or numbers).

   c. Players take turns calling out ordered pairs in an effort to locate the vertices of their opponent's hidden shapes. They say *hit* or *miss* after each of their opponent's guesses, and draw an *O* for a hit or an *X* for a miss at each of those points on the *My Shapes* grid. Likewise, the opponent draws an *O* or *X* at those coordinates on his or her *My Opponent's Shapes* grid to keep track of hits and misses.

978-1-4129-5926-1

d. If a player calls out a point on the side of a shape instead of a vertex, then that's a "side swipe" and is marked with a solid dot instead of *O* or *X*.

e. When a player successfully hits the last vertex of a shape, his or her opponent announces *hit and captured*, and both players connect the dots, color in that shape on their grid, and write the name of the shape inside the shape.

f. To win the game, players must correctly locate and name all of their opponent's shapes. If they are not sure of a name, they may use their math textbook to check before revealing their paper to their opponent.

3. Monitor students as they set up and play the game. Encourage them to draw shapes in a variety of orientations and in different quadrants of the coordinate grid.

4. After the game, invite students to share the strategies they used to locate their opponent's shapes.

Variations of the Game

- Play a class version of the game in which teams take turns naming ordered pairs to try to locate the hidden shapes you have drawn on a coordinate grid on the board or on an overhead. Make a reference of your shapes ahead of time.

- Encourage more advanced students to incorporate *translation* (sliding a shape to a new position by adding or subtracting the same amount of *x* or *y* to each original value to get the exact same shape in a new location). For example:

Original Positions: *A* (2, 4), *B* (−4, −2), *C* (4, −2)

Translation: (x, y) → (x + 3, y − 1)

New Positions: *A´* (5, 3), *B´* (−1, −3), *C´* (7, −3)

- Players may also connect the shapes to make a solid figure (e.g., triangular prism).

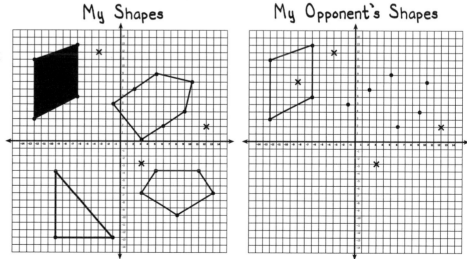

My Shapes   My Opponent's Shapes

Name _____ Date _____

Coordinate Battle-Shapes

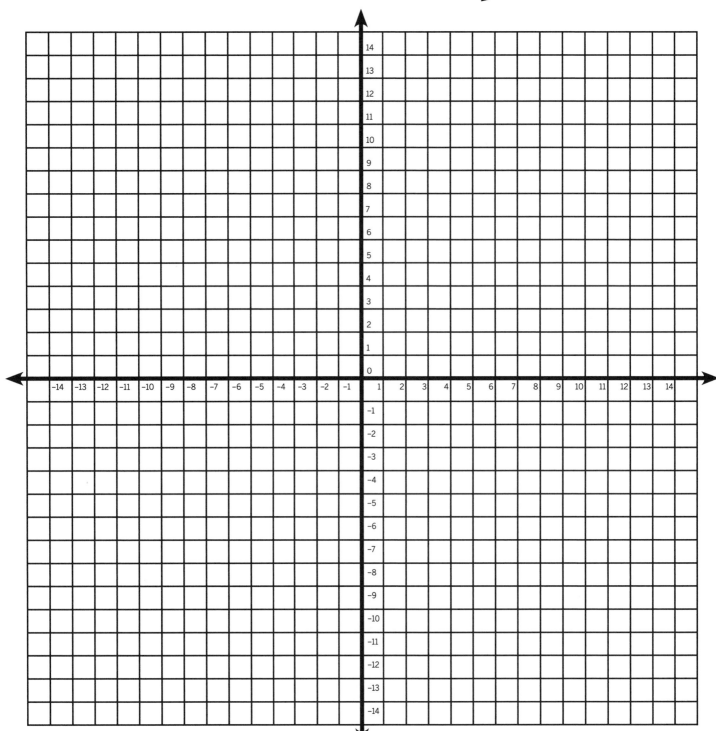

CHAPTER 4

Measurement

Road Builders

Objective

Students will draw and measure line segments and angles.

In this game, players build roadways for a town by drawing line segments according to specific "road rules" of construction. They earn points equal to the lengths of their roads and the angles in between, as long as they can stay on line.

1. Divide the class into groups of three or four students. Give each group a copy of the **Road Builders reproducible (pages 67)** and the supplies needed for the game.

2. Read the directions aloud, and check for understanding before having each group play the game on their own. Make sure students know how to use a ruler and protractor to draw, label, and measure line segments and angles.

   a. Players label each building a different letter, such as *A, B, C, D, E, F, G*, or use the first letter of the building's name.

   b. Players take turns drawing a "road" (line segment) connecting two of the buildings. They write their initials on the road, measure the road, measure the angle between adjacent roads (if applicable), and record that amount for their score.

   c. Players must follow these "road rules" of construction when drawing roads:
      - A road cannot cross another road.
      - A road cannot pass through a building. (All roads must stop or end at a building.)
      - No building can have more than three roads going to or away from it.

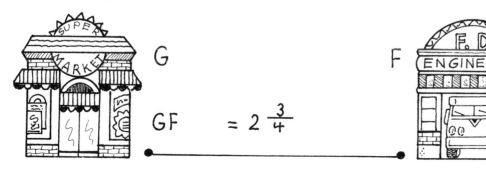

$GF = 2\frac{3}{4}$

d. If players draw a road adjacent to one of their other roads, they earn the value of the angle between those two roads in addition to the length of the new road.

e. Players may also draw and label a "new building" (a dot) anywhere along a previously drawn road, and then draw their new road from that place to another place.

f. The game ends when a player draws an incorrect road (does not follow the road rules). Whichever of the remaining players has the greatest total points wins.

3. Monitor students as they play the game, making sure they are measuring correctly and following the rules of the game.

4. After students play the game, invite them to share and discuss their strategies.

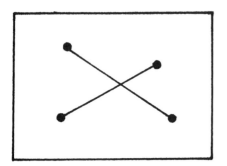 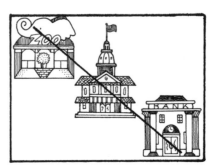 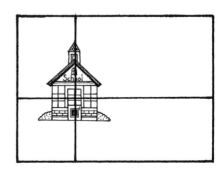

Incorrect Moves, Not Allowed in the Game

Variations of the Game

• Instruct students to include estimation in the game, awarding five extra points to any player that estimates within 1/2 inch (one centimeter) or five degrees of the actual measure of a line segment or angle between two adjacent line segments.

• Have students cut out and glue the buildings from the reproducible onto butcher paper to make a larger game sheet. Have students "build a town" as they play the game, drawing and measuring outlines of new buildings below their dots.

978-1-4129-5926-1

Road Builders

Conversion Match-Up

Objective
Students will identify and match equivalent units of measurement using both customary and metric units of length, weight, and capacity.

This mathematical game of recall and memorization offers students the opportunity to practice their conversion skills. This simple, yet challenging activity is played similarly to the popular commercial game *Concentration*® (a registered trademark of NBC Universal, Inc.).

1. Divide the class into groups of two or three students. Display the following conversions on the board for each group to copy onto 60 separate index cards, with half of each equation on a separate card (e.g., *1 foot* on one card, *12 inches* on another). Review the meanings of the abbreviations.

Length	Weight/Mass	Capacity
1 ft = 12 in	1 kg = 1,000 g	1 tbsp = 3 tsp
1 yd = 3 ft	1 g = 100 cg	1 c = 16 tbsp
1 mi = 5,280 ft	1 g = 10 dg	1 pt = 2 c
1 mi = 1,760 yd	1 g = 1,000 mg	1 qt = 2 pt
1 m = 1,000 mm	1 lb = 16 oz	1 gal = 4 qt
1 m = 100 cm	1 lb = 0.5 kg	1 L = 1,000 mL
1 m = 10 dm	1 t = 2,000 lb	1 kL = 1,000 L
1 dm = 10 cm		1 oz = 28.4 g
1 cm = 10 mm		1 qt = 0.9 L
1 km = 1,000 m		
1 in = 2.5 cm		
1 mi = 1.6 km		
1 ft = 30.5 cm		
1 yd = 0.9 m		

2. Explain and demonstrate how to play the game:
   a. Players shuffle the cards and place them facedown in rows of six (6 x 10 array).
   b. They take turns flipping over a pair of cards to see if the cards match. If the cards match, they keep the cards and turn over another pair. If the cards do not match, they turn the cards back over and the game continues with the next player.

c. The object of the game is for players to not only make matches and collect cards, but also to try and remember where they have seen cards before so they can find them again.

d. The player with the most cards at the end of the game wins.

3. Monitor students as they play. Point out that some cards have more than one match, such as *1 ft = 12 in = 30.5 cm*, but players may match only two cards.

4. After students finish playing the game, invite them to share what they have learned and to suggest ways to modify or enhance the game. Challenge students to discuss the pros and cons of the metric system and whether or not the United States should convert from the customary system to the metric system.

Variations of the Game

- Have students make more cards, including conversions such as *3 feet = 36 inches*.

- Suggest making "geometric" cards to include in the game or to play as a separate Geometric Match-Up game. Have students include pairs of congruent angles in different orientations (flipped, rotated), complementary angles (sum of 90°), supplementary angles (sum of 180°), and similar polygons. Provide them with measuring tools to draw each pair of shapes on separate cards.

- For a greater challenge, have students create and play Word Problem Match-Up, in which they write pairs of word problems and answers on separate cards. Consider providing them with word problems and answers.

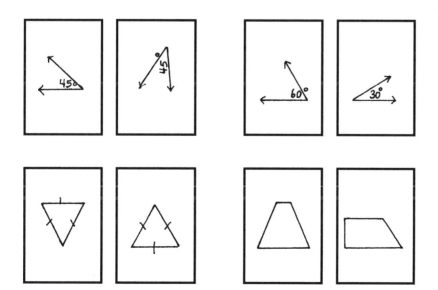

Building a Better Bridge

Materials
- round, pointed toothpicks
- modeling clay
- glue
- metric rulers
- gram weights
- tweezers

Objective
Students will build and measure the length and holding capacity of a model bridge.

In this competitive game, students work in teams to construct the longest and the strongest bridge of toothpicks according to specific standards of construction. They will use their measurement skills and their architectural creativity as they compete to build the best bridge.

1. Divide the class into teams and explain the goal of the game—work with a team to build the longest and strongest bridge of toothpicks using specific regulations.

2. Display the following regulations and read them aloud. Explain that the most important goal is to make the bridge as sturdy as possible so it can hold the most weight. Caution students not to make the bridge so long that it might fall apart.

Bridge Construction Regulations
- You may only use round toothpicks (no flat toothpicks), modeling clay, and glue to build your bridge.
- You cannot glue toothpicks together side by side. They must cross each other or attach end to end.
- Bridges should be at least 50 centimeters long and 5 centimeters wide. (Use a ruler to measure as you build.) There is no height limit.
- There must be a flat part in the center of the bridge for adding weight (to test its strength).

3. Monitor teams as they build their bridges, reminding them to follow the rules of construction. Encourage them to devise a plan and assign specific responsibilities to each teammate before they begin construction.

978-1-4129-5926-1

4. After allowing the bridges to dry overnight, invite each team to present their bridge, describing their process for building and explaining why they think it is the best bridge. Instruct teams to prove the length, strength, and durability of their bridges as follows, recording the results on the board for comparison:
   - Invite a volunteer from each team to measure the length and width of the bridge to prove that it meets the size requirements.
   - Have each team estimate how much weight they think their bridge will hold. Test their predictions by having each team take turns placing gram weights, one at a time, on the flat center of their bridge to see how much it can hold.

5. Instruct teams to add their number values to determine who has the top score and the best bridge.

6. Encourage students to discuss the strategies they used while constructing their bridges. Guide the discussion to help students discover why some designs were more successful.

Variations of the Game
- Ask students to include a scale drawing of their bridge next to their model.

- Have teams lay a cardboard strip on top of their toothpick bridge and test its usability by rolling a toy car from one end of the bridge to the other.

- Instead of a bridge, have teams build a toothpick tower, and then compare heights. Or instruct them to build their own toothpick version of the Leaning Tower of Pisa to see whose tower leans at the largest angle without falling over.

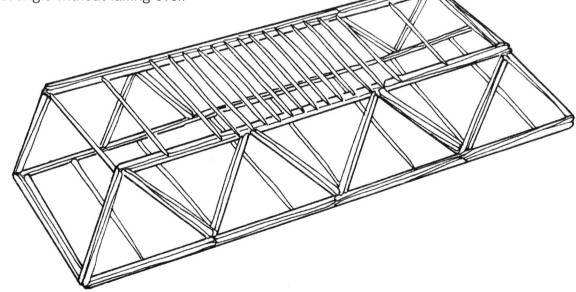

Fearless Flyers

Objective

Students will build and test the efficiency of paper airplanes by measuring and comparing surface area, flight distance, and duration.

In this activity, students use their measuring skills and creative "aeronautic design" to compete in a flight contest. They will try to design and build a paper airplane that flies longer and farther than their classmates' planes.

1. Give students a sheet of 8 1/2" x 14" copy paper to make a paper airplane without the use of tape, paper clips, or staples. Students can follow the directions on the **Building a Paper Airplane reproducible (page 74)**, or they can create their own unique designs. Have them record how to make the airplane, step by step, in their math journal.

2. Distribute measuring tools (rulers, tape measures, stopwatches) and review with students how to calculate surface area of regular and irregular shapes. Have students measure and record the surface area of their airplane's wings.

3. Take students to a large indoor area, such as an auditorium or a long hallway, to have an airplane flying contest without the effects of wind. Have pairs of students take turns throwing their airplane five times and recording the distance and duration of each flight. Monitor students to make sure their measurements are accurate.

4. Instruct students to calculate the average of their top three values for both distance and duration. Use those results to determine two winners for the game, one for the longest distance and one for the longest duration.

5. Have students graph their results on two class graphs: *Duration of Flight vs. Wing Area* and *Distance vs. Wing Area*. Compare and discuss the results.

Airplane Troubleshooting

- **Flies Downward:** Make the wingtips narrower at the front and wider at the back.

- **Flies Upward and Stalls:** Widen the angle of the wingtips; add downward flaps.

- **Curves to One Side and Dives:** Tilt the plane's body left or right relative to the wings (in the direction you want the plane to go); widen the angle of one of the wingtips (the one opposite of where you want the plane to go); fix any asymmetric folds.

Variations of the Game

Challenge students to design and build better airplanes and explain the reasons for changes in their designs. You might also have them write a summary of their results and variables tested. Possible modifications: Make the wings bigger; make the wings smaller; spread the wings farther apart; fold and reposition the wing flaps or tail.

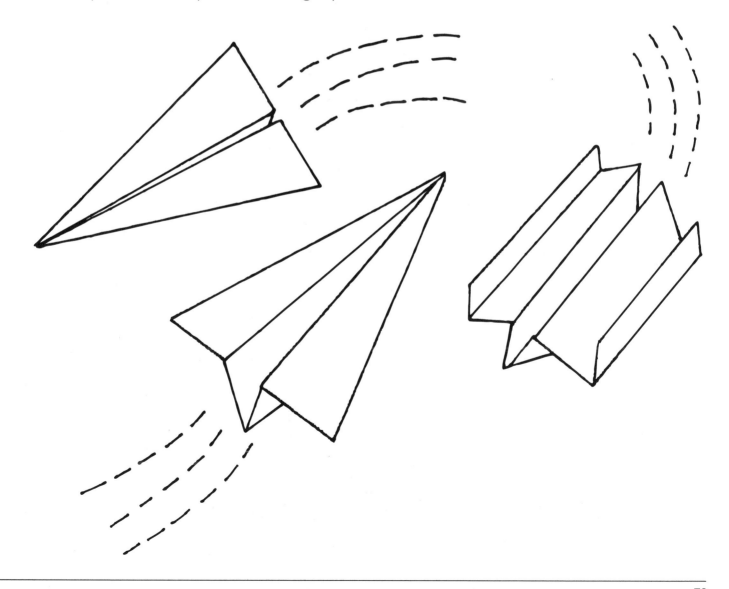

Name _____   Date _____

Building a Paper Airplane

Directions: Follow these steps to make your paper airplane.

Begin with an 8½" x 14" sheet of paper.			**Step 1** Fold over top right corner.
Reverse side	**Turn over paper**	**Fold line**	**Crease line** ... **Fold in this direction**

Step 2 Unfold.	**Step 3** Fold over top left corner.	**Step 4** Unfold.	**Step 5** Turn over paper.

Step 6 Fold down top of paper to meet crease line.	**Step 7** Unfold.	**Step 8** Turn over paper.	**Step 9** Push sides in at fold line, then pull top down.

Step 10 Turn over paper.	**Step 11** Fold top down.	**Step 12** Fold over top right corner to center.	**Step 13** Fold over top left corner to center.

Step 14 Fold up tip.	**Step 15** Turn over paper.	**Step 16** Fold in half.	**Step 17** Rotate paper.

Step 18 Fold over front flap.	**Step 19** Fold over back flap.	**Step 20** Fold up both flaps.	Take off!

Hot Rod Relay Race

Objective

Students will convert metric and customary units of measure.

In this game, teams convert metric and customary units of measure as they participate in a hot rod relay race.

1. Make an enlarged copy of the **Hot Rod Parts** and **Hot Rod Factory reproducibles (pages 76–77)** for each team, and display the factory sheets side by side in a large area for a relay.

2. Tell students that they will be part of a team competing in a "hot rod" relay. In the relay, they will convert parts of a European hot rod into an American version (converting metric units to customary units of measure). Instruct each team to cut out their hot rod parts (including the part name and weight) and glue them onto separate sticky notes.

3. Instruct teams to put their sticky notes facedown next to the starting line of the relay and line up for the race. When you say *go*, the first player on each team takes a car part, calculates the conversion (rounded to the nearest whole number), and races to the team's factory chart, matching the part's metric mass to the corresponding customary weight.

4. The player then runs back to his or her team and tags the next person in line, who continues the relay. Each player can move only one car part at a time, either putting a new part on the chart, or moving a mismatched part to its correct position.

5. The first team to correctly place all of their car parts into their factory wins.

Variations of the Game

- Instruct students to estimate the amounts before they calculate the conversions.

- Include an obstacle course as part of the relay.

- Have students convert other kinds of measurements, such as the length (metric to customary) and prices (Euros to dollars) of different car parts.

Materials
- Hot Rod Parts reproducible
- Hot Rod Factory reproducible
- scissors
- glue sticks
- large sticky notes

Name _____ Date _____

Hot Rod Parts

Directions: Convert the metric measurements to customary measurements (given 1 kg = 2.2 lbs.). Round answers to the nearest whole number, if needed.

Engine: 400 kg

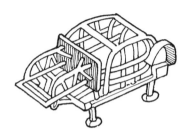

Frame: 160 kg

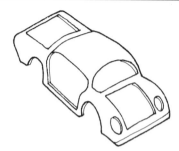

Body Shell: 509 kg

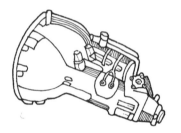

Transmission: 60 kg

Front Grill: 5.5 kg

Tire: 18.2 kg

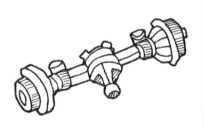

Rear Axle: 43.2 kg

Steering Set: 8.2 kg

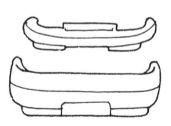

Bumpers: 11.8 kg

Door and Trunk Lid: 55 kg

Car Seat: 11.4 kg

Set of Windows: 40 kg

Reproducible   978-1-4129-5926-1 • © Corwin Press

Hot Rod Factory

18 lbs.	88 lbs.	40 lbs.
26 lbs.	25 lbs.	132 lbs.
121 lbs.	1,120 lbs.	95 lbs.
12 lbs.	352 lbs.	880 lbs.

Geo-Measure Scavenger Hunt

Materials

- Geo-Measure Scavenger Hunt reproducible
- writing paper
- clipboards
- measuring tools (metric rulers, protractors, measuring cups, balance scale)

Objective

Students will apply their knowledge of measurement and geometry to find examples of items listed for a scavenger hunt.

Invite students to go on a mathematical scavenger hunt! Using their knowledge of measurement and geometry, along with a little bit of detective work, they will compete to find the mystery objects.

1. Give each team of students a copy of the **Geo-Measure Scavenger Hunt reproducible (page 79)** and writing paper clipped to a clipboard (record sheet). Or, give students a copy of your own list of math-related items to hunt for.

2. Have each team start on a different number of the Geo-Measure Scavenger Hunt list (e.g., Team 1 on item 1, Team 2 on item 5, and so on). Teammates must search for the same item together; they may not split up and search for different items. On their record sheet, they must list the object's name and location, the estimated measurement, and the actual measurement.

3. Before students begin the scavenger hunt, you might want to review some rules and expectations, such as reminding them to stay within school boundaries, not to disturb other classes in session, and to be careful and respectful of the items they are measuring.

4. Set a time limit for students to find the items. Monitor students as they complete the scavenger hunt, making sure they are staying on task. Award points for each item they find (more points for more challenging items). The team with the greatest total points wins the scavenger hunt.

Variation of the Game

Have students collect the smaller items in resealable bags and/or take pictures of the items found for the scavenger hunt. Consider having students create a poster of their pictured items and award extra points for their presentation.

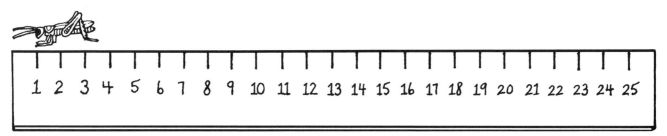

Name _____ Date _____

Geo-Measure Scavenger Hunt

Directions: Look for examples of these items around campus. Use measuring tools to calculate and record your results.

1. Something that is between 3 and 5 centimeters long.

2. Something that is about twice the length of your foot.

3. A container that holds between 100 and 120 milliliters.

4. Something that weighs more than 5 kilograms but less than 10 kilograms.

5. Something that has more than three acute angles.

6. Perimeter and area of a school sign or plaque, and the name of its shape.

7. Height of your math teacher.

8. Rectangular prism whose volume is greater than its surface area.

9. Total volume of a student's locker and the maximum number of identical math textbooks that could fit inside.

10. Surface area of a school bench.

11. Area of classroom floor and the number of 4 x 6 tiles needed to cover that area.

12. The cost to carpet the library floor (carpet = $18.98 per yard; pad = $7.98 per yard).

13. Area of a regular hexagon or octagon found outside math class.

14. Perimeter and area of a student's desk (measured to the nearest eighth inch and converted to metric units).

15. Length of the longest last name in class (typed using 14-point Times New Roman font and then measured to the nearest tenth of a centimeter).

16. Circumference, area, and volume of a spherical ball.

17. Dimensions of a piece of playground equipment taller than 6 feet.

18. Perimeter and area of the football field or other large grass area.

19. Average distance your team can jump in a "long jump."

20. Bonus! The Fibonacci sequence begins with *1, 1, 2, 3, 5, . . .* After the two starting values, each number is the sum of the two preceding numbers. It identifies itself with nature. Find something in nature to show the sequence.

CHAPTER 5

Data Analysis and Probability

Out on a Limb

<table>
<tr><td></td><td>Player 1</td><td>stem</td><td>Player 2</td></tr>
</table>

Materials
- Out on a Limb reproducible
- Spinner reproducible
- large paper clips
- pencils
- overhead projector and transparency

Objective
Students will make and use a stem-and-leaf plot to identify different measures of central tendency for a random set of data.

For this game, players spin for numbers and plot them on their side of a double stem-and-leaf plot. The goal is to obtain the greatest mean, median, and mode.

1. Review with students how to find the mean, median, and mode for a given set of values, and review how to plot two-digit numbers on a stem-and-leaf plot.

2. Give each pair of students a copy of the **Out on a Limb reproducible (page 81)** and two copies of the Spinner reproducible (page 11). Have students make a "tens" spinner by numbering the sections *0–90*, by tens, and a "ones" spinner by numbering the sections *0–9*.

3. Read the directions aloud and have a volunteer help you demonstrate how to play the game on an overhead transparency. Show how to spin the spinners with a paper clip and pencil, and record the two-digit numbers on the stem-and-leaf plot. Explain that after ten turns, players find the mean, median, and mode of their ten values and earn up to three points, one point each for a mean, median, or mode greater than their opponent's. The player with the most points wins the game.

4. Monitor students as they play the game three times. Check that they are plotting the values correctly and are using only one stem-and-leaf plot for each game.

5. After a few games, discuss with the class the effects that certain numbers had on the mean, median, and mode of their data sets.

Player 1 / Player 2 (double stem-and-leaf plot)

Player 1	stem	Player 2
	0	8
5	1	3, 4
7, 1, 1	2	
6	3	
9	4	5, 9, 9
	5	
	6	0
4, 3	7	
	8	1, 1, 8
8, 2	9	

Variation of the Game
Have students play a decimal version of the game, adding decimal points to create a "stem" of tenths and "leaves" of hundredths.

978-1-4129-5926-1

Out on a Limb

How to Play: Take turns spinning the Tens and Ones spinners to make a two-digit number and plot it on your side of the Stem-and-Leaf Plot. After ten turns, find the mean, median, and mode of your ten values. You earn one point each for a mean, median, or mode that is greater than your opponent's. The player with the most points wins the game!

Game 1

Player 1 | Player 2

| 0 |
| 1 |
| 2 |
| 3 |
| 4 |
| 5 |
| 6 |
| 7 |
| 8 |
| 9 |

Game 2

Player 1 | Player 2

| 0 |
| 1 |
| 2 |
| 3 |
| 4 |
| 5 |
| 6 |
| 7 |
| 8 |
| 9 |

Game 3

Player 1 | Player 2

| 0 |
| 1 |
| 2 |
| 3 |
| 4 |
| 5 |
| 6 |
| 7 |
| 8 |
| 9 |

Math Baseball

Materials

- Baseball Statistics reproducible
- index cards
- assorted math problems (four different levels of difficulty)
- baseball statistics (from newspapers, baseball cards, and online sources)

Objective

Students will explore real-world math connections, interpreting statistical data about baseball using computation of whole numbers, decimals, and fractions.

In this in-class version of baseball, students answer a variety of math questions to score hits and home runs. Students will hone their math skills by solving real-world problems interpreting baseball statistics.

1. Use index cards to make four decks of math problems, one question per card, with each deck containing an increasing level of difficulty in accordance with its hit designation (single, double, triple, home run). Include math problems from the class textbook as well as some from baseball statistics, such as those on the **Baseball Statistics reproducible (page 84)**. Give students a copy of the reproducible to use as a reference during the game.

2. Divide the class into two teams and prepare a lineup roster of batters for each team. A "batter" can be one student or a pair of students working together.

3. Explain to the class that a team is at bat until all players have taken a turn or until the team gets three outs. Each batter tells you what kind of "hit" he or she would like (single, double, triple, home run) before you read it aloud. The batter must respond within one minute and can say only one answer. If the answer is correct, the batter earns that hit; if not, the team gets an out.

4. The batter and all base runners advance the number of bases corresponding to the hit made by the batter. For example, if a batter singles with runners on second and third bases, the runner on third scores, the runner on second goes to third, and the batter goes to first base.

5. If a batter is stumped by a question, he or she may opt for a "sacrifice," in which the team can help him or her answer the question. If he or she is correct, all runners except the batter advance and an "out" is still recorded for the batter.

6. The first team to earn ten runs, or the team with the most runs after nine innings, wins!

Variation of the Game

Play outdoor math baseball, having batters solve a math problem before they take their turn at bat. If they answer the question incorrectly, it counts as one strike, leaving only two more strikes for their turn at bat.

Sample Baseball Statistics Questions

- What is a player's BA (batting average) if he or she hit "25 for 62"? *(.403)*

- If a player gets 25 hits—4 doubles, 0 triples, and 5 home runs—how many singles (1B) did that player get? *(16 singles)*

- What is the TB (total bases) for a player with the following hits: 8 singles, 3 doubles, 1 triple, 2 home runs? *(25 bases)*

- What is the SLG (slugging percentage) for a player with the following stats: 100 at bats, 26 hits, 5 doubles, 2 triples, 4 home runs? *(.470)*

- What is the number of hits for a player with a BA = .250 in 120 at bats? *(30 hits)*

- If a player ended the season with 18 doubles, 1 triple, and 56 home runs, how many total bases (TB) does he or she have, without counting singles? *(263 total bases)*

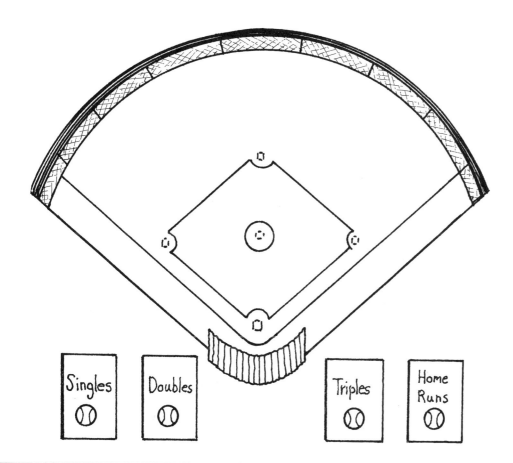

Baseball Statistics

Directions: Use the following statistical formulas to answer math problems related to baseball.

Sample Baseball Statistics

Player	TEAM	G	AB	R	H	2B	3B	HR	RBI	TB	BB	SO	SB	CS	OBP	SLG	AVG
1. M. Carrera	TX	18	62	12	25	4	0	5	18	44	11	9	1	0	.500	.710	.403
2. J. Monroe	MIN	19	69	16	27	9	0	0	9	36	10	10	3	0	.469	.522	.391
3. C. Williams	FLA	17	67	22	26	5	2	3	6	44	11	12	6	1	.488	.657	.388
4. H. Juarez	NYM	21	85	10	33	6	1	2	11	47	7	17	2	0	.435	.553	.388
5. A. Blaze	CIN	19	78	26	30	7	0	14	34	79	8	20	1	0	.444	1.013	.385

G: Games Played, AB: At Bats, R: Runs Scored, H: Hits, 2B: Doubles, 3B: Triples, HR: Home Runs, RBI: Runs Batted In, TB: Total Bases, BB: Bases on Balls (Walks), SO: Strikeouts, SB: Stolen Bases, CS: Caught Stealing, OBP: On-Base Percentage, SLG: Slugging Percentage, AVG: Batting Average

Baseball Calculations

Batting Average: BA = H ÷ AB, written as a three-digit decimal.
[Batting Average (BA) = Hits (H) divided by At Bats (AB)]

Slugging Percentage: (SLG) = TB ÷ AB, written as a three-digit decimal.
[Slugging Percentage (SLG) = Total Base Hits (TB) divided by At Bats (AB); where TB = (1 × number of singles) + (2 × number of doubles) + (3 × number of triples) + (4 × number of home runs)]

Example: The BA for "1 hit for 4 at bats" = 1 ÷ 4 = .250.

To calculate the BA over two games, divide the sums of "hits" by "at bats."

Example: The BA for "1 for 4" and "3 for 5" = (1 + 3) ÷ (4 + 5) = 4 ÷ 9 = .444.

Example: For 3 hits in 8 at bats ("3 for 8"), with two singles and one triple:
SLG = [(1 × 2) + (3 × 1)] ÷ 8 At Bats = 5 ÷ 8 = .625.

High or Low?

Objective

Students will use probability, data analysis, and deductive reasoning to make decisions during a game.

Materials
• decks of playing cards

In this game, players try to choose one of three facedown cards with a value greater than a card on display. They will use their knowledge of probability and tally charts to help them decide which card to keep and which to replace.

1. Before playing the game, review how to calculate probability (independent and dependent). For example, ask: *If 12 of 52 cards have been discarded, and none of those cards are jacks, what is the probability that the next card is a jack? (P = 4:40 = 1:10)*

2. Divide the class into pairs of students, and have each student make a tally chart showing the 13 categories of numbers and face cards in the deck (*2, 3, 4, 5, 6, 7, 8, 9, 10, J, Q, K, A*).

3. Explain the rules of the game and demonstrate with a volunteer:
   a. Player 1 places four cards from the deck facedown in a row, without looking at them, and then turns over the first card.
   b. Player 2 selects one of the facedown cards, without revealing it, and uses probability to decide whether to keep that card or to discard it and select a different facedown card. The goal is to choose a card with the greatest value.
   c. If Player 2 keeps the first card, Player 1 may choose between the two remaining facedown cards. If Player 2 selects a different card, Player 1 must take the last facedown card.
   d. Both players reveal their cards. Whoever has a card with a greater value than the faceup card keeps all four cards. If both players' cards are greater, then the player with the greatest value keeps the cards. If neither players' cards are greater, the cards are discarded and no one gets them.
   e. Players draw tally marks to record the cards that have been used, so they can determine the probability of getting each of the remaining cards in the next round.
   f. Players switch roles and play again with the next four cards from the deck, using their tally charts and probability to help them make decisions.
   g. Players continue taking turns until the entire deck is used. The player with the most cards at the end of the game wins!

Math Quiz Show

Materials
- poster board
- letter envelopes
- scissors
- tape or glue
- colored markers
- index cards
- noisemakers or bells
- stopwatch

Objective
Students will use a variety of math skills and strategies to solve assorted math problems, including data analysis and real-world application.

This game is played similarly to the popular game show *Jeopardy*® (a registered trademark of Jeopardy Productions, Inc. dba Merv Griffin Enterprises Corporation). It can be used to review concepts in all different math categories.

1. Make a Math Quiz Show board by using letter-sized envelopes cut in half to create pockets and attaching those pockets in a 5 x 5 array on poster board. Write column headers such as *Number and Operations, Algebra, Geometry, Measurement,* and *Data Analysis and Probability.* Label each column of pockets *100, 200, 300, 400, 500* (point values) from top to bottom.

2. Make game cards for each category by writing math problems on separate index cards (see pages 87–88). Put them in the pockets by level of difficulty. Hide two "Daily Double" cards behind two cards to double their point value.

3. Write the problems in the form of an answer, and have players respond in the form of a question, similar to the game show. For example:

   Game Card: *It is the prime factorization of 1,325.*

   Response: *What is 5, 5, 53?*

4. To play the game, divide the class into teams and give each team a noisemaker or bell to "buzz in" with the correct answer. Choose a team to go first and have that team choose a problem from the game board by category and point value (e.g., *Measurement for 300 points*). Practice with a few game cards, and allow each team one practice round.

5. Read the answer aloud. The first team to buzz in gets the first chance to respond. If they respond correctly, they win that number of points and choose the next card. If they answer incorrectly, or take longer than five seconds to respond, they lose that number of points from their score and the other teams get a chance to buzz in with the correct response.

6. Before you begin playing a real game, remind students that they must respond with questions, not answers. If they do not, they lose a turn.

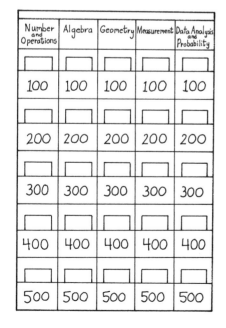

Number and Operations	Algebra	Geometry	Measurement	Data Analysis and Probability
100	100	100	100	100
200	200	200	200	200
300	300	300	300	300
400	400	400	400	400
500	500	500	500	500

7. Have a scorekeeper from each team keep track of his or her team's score on the board, including negative totals if the team loses more points than earned. The team with the most points at the end of the game wins!

Variation of the Game

Make a second set of "double points" questions and a "final" question. Teams must decide how many points to wager before the final card is read.

Sample Quiz Show Cards

Number and Operations

- It is the next number in the pattern: *2 1 4 3 6 5 8 7. (Answer: 10)*

- It is the prime factorization of 1,325. *(Answer: 5 × 5 × 53)*

- It is the solution of –11/12 – (–5/3). *(Answer: 3/4)*

- Zack calls Nicole at 5:43 p.m. and talks until 6:12 p.m. If Zack pays 23 cents for each minute, it is the total cost of his phone call to Nicole. *(Answer: $6.67)*

- Maria's lunch costs $10.60. She leaves a 15% tip. This is the total amount of her bill. *(Answer: $10.60 + $1.59 = $12.19 total)*

Algebra

- It is the solution of the function $f(x) = 3x + 2$ when $x = –3$. *(Answer: –7)*

- For the equation $3 + (1/5)x = –10$, it is the value of x. *(Answer: x = –65)*

- For the inequality $3x – 9 > 12$, it is the solution for x. *(Answer: x > 7)*

- It is the simplified solution of $(2x^2)^3 (–x^4)$. *(Answer: –8x^{10})*

- It is the solution to the quadratic equation $x^2 – 11x + 30$. *(Answer: x = 6, 5)*

Geometry

- It is the specific name of a triangle with sides measuring 5 cm, 7 cm, 9 cm, and with angles measuring 54°, 49°, 77°. *(Answer: scalene acute triangle)*

- It is the length of the base of a right triangle with an altitude of 12 inches and a hypotenuse of 20 inches. *(Answer: b = 16 inches)*

- These measurements are the circumference and area of a circle, respectively, with a diameter of 6 feet and using 3.14 for π. *(Answer: C = 18.84 ft; A = 28.26 ft²)*

- It is the volume of a cone, rounded to the nearest foot, with a height of 8 feet, a radius of 4 feet, and using 3.14 for π. *(Answer: V = 134 ft³)*

- It is the surface area of a rectangular prism with length of 3 centimeters, width of 2 centimeters, and height of 5 centimeters. *(Answer: 62 cm²)*

Measurement

- It is the amount of money you will pay for four melons that are 8 ounces each and one dollar per pound. *(Answer: $2.00)*

- Kyle leaves his house at 7:00 a.m. He drives for 28 miles and suddenly remembers he left the oven on. He turns around and drives home to turn off the oven. If he drives 57 miles to his destination, it is the total miles he has driven. *(Answer: 113 miles)*

- If a battery-operated car can go 45 miles per hour, it is the length of time it will take to drive to a destination 320 miles away. *(Answer: = 7 hours, 7 minutes)*

- It is the number of yards, rounded to the nearest hundredth, a glider travels if it flies a distance of 389 feet. *(Answer: 129.67 yards)*

- If 563 million gallons of milk are consumed in a year, how many gallons are consumed in a day if the amount per day is the same? *(Answer: 1,542,465.75 gallons)*

Data Analysis and Probability

- It is your mean score if you receive the following scores on math exams: 85, 67, 92, 64, 81, 77, 73. *(Answer: 77)*

- There is one penny, one nickel, and one dime in a bag. It is the probability that you will pull out a penny and a dime if you pull out two coins. *(Answer: P = 1/3)*

- It is the next pair of numbers in this number pattern: *(14, 7), (24, 17), (34, 27). (Answer: 44, 37)*

- It is the number of different outfits you can make with three pairs of pants, six T-shirts, and two pairs of shoes. *(Answer: 36 outfits)*

- You have a bag containing four red marbles and three yellow marbles. You want to take two marbles out of the bag. If the first marble is not put back into the bag before the second one is taken out, it is the probability that both marbles are red. *(Answer: P = 2/7)*

978-1-4129-5926-1

Stock Market Math

Objective

Students will apply their math skills to create a stock portfolio and trade stocks.

In Stock Market Math, students explore real-world mathematics by investing a hypothetical $100,000 in stock market purchases. They research and evaluate actual companies, simulate buying and selling stocks, and use their math skills to calculate costs and track earnings as they compete to be the "top investor."

1. Invite students to share what they know about the stock market and buying stocks. Explain that they will work in teams to invest a hypothetical $100,000, for one month. They will compete against each other to see who can make the best investments and earn the most money.

2. Discuss how the stock market works, explaining how, where, and why people buy stocks (shares of ownership in a company). Include the following facts:

   • There are three main stock markets in the United States: *New York Stock Exchange (NYSE)*, the largest organized stock market in the United States, used by larger national companies; *American Stock Exchange (AMEX)*, also located in New York City, lists data for smaller and energy-related companies; *Nasdaq Stock Market (NASDAQ)*, the choice of many high-technology companies, trading exclusively through electronic communication.

   • The price, or value, of a stock continuously changes throughout the day, from opening to closing (4:00 p.m. ET). The price reflects the interest of investors and the economy, changing as supply and demand changes. The goal is to make a profit by buying stocks when the prices are low and then selling when the prices are high.

Materials

- Stock Market Examples reproducible
- Stock Market Definitions reproducible
- Stock Market Trading Sheet reproducible
- Stock Market Progress Sheet reproducible
- newspaper stock tables or Internet stock sites
- binders or report folders
- large chart-sized graph paper
- colored pencils or thin markers
- calculators

3. Give students a copy of the **Stock Market Examples** and **Stock Market Definitions reproducibles (pages 91–92)** and discuss the information with them. Ask questions to check for understanding.

4. Give each team copies of the **Stock Market Trading Sheet** and **Stock Market Progress Sheet reproducibles (pages 93–94)**, and use overhead transparencies to guide instruction. Explain and demonstrate how to complete each chart. Have teams keep their copies (and subsequent copies) in a binder or report folder to make a portfolio of their investments.

5. Instruct students to brainstorm a list of popular brand names to get started (e.g., food, clothing, athletic equipment, hotels, cars, airlines), generating a list of possible companies for their investments. For each company they choose, have teams record the following data and explain why they chose that stock: company name, parent company, name of stock, ticker symbol, summary of company's products, company's strengths and weaknesses (in comparison to their competitors), and research references. Encourage students to use online resources, such as Hoover's Online Research at: *www.hoovers.com/free*.

6. Encourage teams to buy or sell stocks at least twice a week and record their transactions in their portfolio. They may use daily newspapers from home or online resources such as those listed below. Set a minimum of 100 shares per transaction. Consider excluding "penny stocks" (those less than five dollars per share).
   - Yahoo Financial Investment Site: *http://finance.yahoo.com*
   - New York Stock Exchange: *www.nyse.com*
   - American Stock Exchange: *www.amex.com*
   - Nasdaq Stock Exchange: *www.nasdaq.com*

7. Have the class monitor and compare their progress by creating a large multiple-line graph (dollars vs. date), on which each team graphs the total value of their portfolio every day or every other day. Ask each team to graph their results in a different color.

8. Assess each team's progress and portfolio at least once a week, making sure they are working cooperatively and completing the record sheets correctly. After one month, announce the winners. The team with the most money wins.

978-1-4129-5926-1

Stock Market Examples

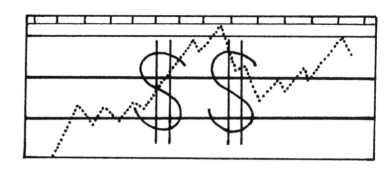

Newspaper Example

| Stock | Sym | 52-Week | | Day's | | Div | Yld % | P/E | Vol 100s | Close | Net Chg |
		Hi	Lo	Hi	Lo						
Funland	FUN	66.85	37.25	63.50	59.35	1.04	1.7	26	12725	61.50	−1.75

Internet Example

BRIGHT LIFE ENERGY COMPANY (NYSE: BL) Delayed Quote Data

Last Trade:	**37.01**	Day's Range:	36.02 – 37.02
Trade Time:	2:02 PM ET	52wk Range:	32.06 – 38.49
Change:	↑ **1.17 (3.26%)**	Volume:	62,199,914
Prev Close:	35.84	Avg Vol (3m):	34,425,700
Open:	36.10	Market Cap:	380.58B
Bid:	N/A	P/E:	18.34
Ask:	N/A	EPS:	2.02
1y Target Est:	42.00	Div & Yield:	1.12 (3.20%)

BL 16–Apr 2:02pm

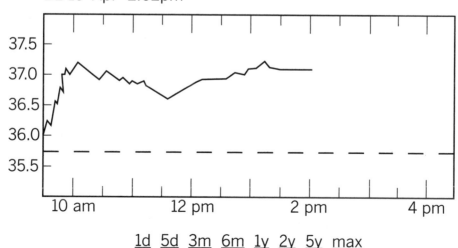

1d 5d 3m 6m 1y 2y 5y max

Stock Market Definitions

52-Week Hi & Lo: The highest and lowest prices of the stock during the last 52 weeks. (Some sources only list the daily hi & lo or "daily range.")

Change or Net Change (Net Chg): The difference between a stock's closing (or last) price on a given day and its closing price on the previous trading day.

Common Stocks: The basic ownership of a company, owning most of the company's profits and bearing most of its losses. They have no guaranteed dividend.

Dividend (Div): Part of a company's profits (earnings) that it pays to stockholders.

Earnings Per Share (EPS): A company's profits (total earnings) divided equally among all the shares sold to investors (outstanding shares): *total earnings ÷ no. of outstanding shares.*

Last or Close: The most recent (last) trading price of a stock on a particular day. If the trading day is over, the last price is also the *Closing Price.*

Market Capitalization (Market Cap): The total current market value of all outstanding shares (sold shares): *stock's current price x no. of outstanding shares.*

Preferred Stocks (pf): Stocks with preferred treatment, usually a fixed dividend that must be paid before common stocks can receive any dividends. Should the company go bankrupt, preferred shareholders receive payment prior to common stockholders.

Price/Earnings Ratio (P/E): Indicates how many times greater the stock price is than the earnings per share: *closing price ÷ earnings per share for the latest year.*

Stock Split: Indicated by an *s* after the company's name, it is the division of a stock into a larger number of lower-priced shares, reducing the price per share to encourage sales.

Stock Ticker Symbol (Sym): A one- to four-letter symbol for a company.

Volume (Vol): The total number of shares traded on a given day. For *Vol 100s*, multiply the given value x 100 to get the actual number of shares traded that day.

Yield (Yld %): The amount of dividends received per share of stock compared with the price of that stock, expressed as a percentage: *percentage yield = (dividend per stock ÷ closing price) x 100.*

Name _____ Date _____

Stock Market Trading Sheet

Team Members: _____

Date	Stock Name/Symbol	Buy or Sell?	No. of Shares	Price per Share	Price for All Shares	Broker's Fees (2%)	Total $$ Earned (+) or Spent (–)

Stock Market Progress Sheet

Team Members: _____

Date	Stock Symbol	Current Value of Your Stocks (Price per Share x No. of Shares = Value)	Amount Gain (+) or Loss (−) from Previous Value	Total Current Value of All Stocks (Sum of Current Values)	Total Equity of Your Account (Stocks + Cash Balance) =
					_____ + _____ = _____
					_____ + _____ = _____

Answer Key

FRACTION SPEEDWAY (PAGE 28)
1/4: 3/12, 4/16, 6/24, 8/32, 9/36, 12/48
1/3: 2/6, 4/12, 6/18, 8/24, 9/27, 12/36
2/3: 8/12, 10/15, 12/18, 14/21, 18/27, 24/36
3/4: 6/8, 9/12, 12/16, 24/32, 27/36, 36/48
3/5: 9/15, 12/20, 21/35, 24/40, 27/45, 36/60

FRACTION TIC-TAC-TOE (PAGE 29)
Game 1
$5/9 - 1/6 = 7/18$
$9/10 + 3/4 = 1\ 13/20$
$5/6 + 1/4 = 1\ 1/12$
$12/15 - 1/5 = 3/5$
$3/4 - 2/7 = 13/28$
$1\ 6/7 + 5\ 1/2 = 7\ 5/14$
$2\ 3/5 + 3\ 2/3 = 6\ 4/15$
$5\ 1/8 - 3\ 3/4 = 1\ 3/8$
$7\ 3/4 - 2\ 1/6 = 5\ 7/12$
$3\ 5/16 + 2\ 5/8 = 5\ 15/16$

Game 2
$1\ 2/3 \times 4/5 = 1\ 1/3$
$1/3 \times 3\ 1/2 = 1\ 1/6$
$4\ 2/5 \times 1\ 3/7 = 6\ 2/7$
$4\ 1/12 \times 1\ 3/7 = 5\ 5/6$
$2\ 1/6 \times 3\ 1/3 = 7\ 2/9$
$4\ 1/3 \div 2\ 8/9 = 1\ 1/2$
$4\ 1/6 \div 1\ 2/3 = 2\ 1/2$
$9\ 3/7 \div 5\ 1/2 = 1\ 5/7$
$5\ 1/4 \div 2\ 1/3 = 2\ 1/4$
$2\ 1/7 \div 1\ 2/9 = 1\ 58/77$

Game 3
$3/4 + 1/3 + 5/6 = 1\ 11/12$
$1/4 + 5/8 + 15/16 = 1\ 13/16$
$3/8 + 5/6 + 1/4 = 1\ 11/24$
$3/5 + 8/15 + 1/3 = 1\ 7/15$
$3\ 2/3 - 5/6 \div 5/8 = 2\ 1/3$
$(2/3 + 2/5) \div 1\ 3/5 = 2/3$
$6 \div 2/3 \times 5/18 = 2\ 1/2$
$1/2 \div 3/4 \times 9/10 = 3/5$
$2\ 2/9 \times 3/8 - 1/3 = 1/2$
$6\ 1/3 - 3\ 1/3 \div 1\ 1/4 = 3\ 2/3$

COLOR WHEEL RACE (PAGE 38)

$a = 2.6$	$h = 10.4$	$k = 0.8$	$n = 4.8$
$r = 6.6$	$t = 2.9$	$v = 6.9$	$w = 6.4$
$x = 1.2$	$y = 2.3$	$g = 3.1$	$f = 2.8$
$b = 0.9$	$c = 3.6$	$p = 1.7$	$e = 0.4$

Variations of the Game
Possible pairs that have a sum of 4: *xf, yp, ce, gb*
Possible pairs that differ by 4: *ar, hw, kn, tv*

CAPTURE THE SPY (PAGE 41)
$-5x + 8 = -7; x = 3$
$4x - 3 = 1; x = 1$
$9x + 3 = 48; x = 5$
$6 + x/5 = 7; x = 5$
$14 = 2 + 3x; x = 4$
$-3x + 5 = 5; x = 0$
$-35 = (3 + x)(-5); x = 4$
$3x + 2(x - 6) = -2; x = 2$
$-4(x - 3) = 8; x = 1$
$-2(6 + x) - x = -18; x = 2$
$9(x + 3) - 3x = 39; x = 2$
$5(x - 6) + 3x = -6; x = 3$
$-10 = -4 - x; x = 6$
$13x - 21 = 44; x = 5$
$8x + 22 = 70; x = 6$
$(4/5)x = 3(1/5); x = 3/4$
$(3/8)x = 3/4; x = 2$
$3/x = 81/135; x = 5$

HOT ROD RELAY RACE (PAGES 75–77)
(1 kg ≈ 2.2 lbs.)
Engine: 400 kg = 880 lbs.
Frame: 160 kg = 352 lbs.
Body Shell: 509 kg = 1,120 lbs.
Transmission: 60 kg = 132 lbs.
Front Grill: 5.5 kg = 12 lbs.
Tire: 18.2 kg = 40 lbs.
Rear Axle: 43.2 kg = 95 lbs.
Steering Set: 8.2 kg = 18 lbs.
Bumpers: 11.8 kg = 26 lbs.
Door and Trunk Lid: 55 kg = 121 lbs.
Car Seat: 11.4 kg = 25 lbs.
Set of Windows: 40 kg = 88 lbs.

References

Beyers, J. (1998). The biology of human play. *Child Development, 69*(3), 599–600.

CleverMedia. (1995–2007). *Game scene: Pentominoes.* Retrieved April 30, 2007, from http://gamescene.com/Pentominoes.html.

Games Warehouse. (n.d.). *WebGames: Mastermind.* Retrieved April 30, 2007, from http://www.irt.org/games/js/mind/index.htm.

Gardner, H. (1983). *Frames of mind: The theory of multiple intelligences.* New York, NY: Basic Books.

Hickoksports.com. (n.d.). *Shuffleboard rules.* Retrieved April 30, 2007, from http://www.hickoksports.com/rules/rshuffleb.shtml.

Jensen, E. (2001). *Arts with the brain in mind.* Alexandria, VA: Association for Supervision and Curriculum Development.

Kennedy, P. A., Litwiller, B. H., & Nichols, E. D. (1992). *Holt pre-algebra.* Orlando, FL: Holt, Rinehart and Winston.

McCarthy, B. (1990). Using the 4MAT system to bring learning styles to schools. *Educational Leadership, 48*(2), 31–37.

McLeod, J. (2007, June). *Rules of card games: Gin rummy.* Retrieved April 30, 2007, from the Card Game Web site: http://www.pagat.com/rummy/ginrummy.html.

NASA Glenn Learning Technologies Project. (n.d.). *Paper airplane activity.* Retrieved April 30, 2007, from http://www.grc.nasa.gov/WWW/K-12/TRC/Aeronautics/AeronauticActivitiesHome2.htm.

National Council of Teachers of Mathematics. (2005). *Principles and standards for school mathematics.* Reston, VA: National Council of Teachers of Mathematics (NCTM).

National Council on Economic Education. (1990). *Learning from the market: How to read a stock table.* New York, NY: National Council on Economic Education.

Official Site of Major League Baseball. (n.d.). Retrieved April 30, 2007, from http://mlb.mlb.com/index.jsp.

Tate, M. L. (2003). *Worksheets don't grow dendrites: 20 instructional strategies that engage the brain.* Thousand Oaks, CA: Corwin Press.

Wolfe, P. (2001). *Brain matters: Translating research into classroom practice.* Alexandria, VA: Association for Supervision and Curriculum Development.

Yahoo! Finance. (n.d.). *Investing: Today's markets.* Retrieved April 30, 2007, from http://finance.yahoo.com/marketupdate?